OUT FROM DARKNESS

OUT FROM DARKNESS

Ben Alexander

Out From Darkness (Revised and Expanded Edition)

Copyright 1993 © by Miranda Press

ISBN: 0-963407-10-4

DEDICATED

to my wife Miranda
my son Stewart
and my daughter Mary Victoria

APPRECIATION

I am indebted to many individuals throughout America who have encouraged me to write this book. Without their inspiration I am sure that it would never have been written.

Grateful appreciation is extended to Julia Staton for her suggestions and thoughts.

A special thanks is given to Judy Beltis for her splendid work on the manuscript. I also wish to thank Katherine Plaisted and Laurel Girdwood who worked long hours typing this book. And most of all I wish to thank my wife Miranda for her never failing inspiration and encouragement.

Table of Contents

SECTION I
AUTOBIOGRAPHY

SECTION II
WHAT YOU SHOULD KNOW ABOUT SPIRITUAL DARKNESS

INTRODUCTION
The true story of Ben Alexander
by Knofel Staton

When I received a telephone call asking me to write the Introduction to Ben Alexander's book, *Out From Darkness,* I thought to myself, "Oh no, not another project. I am just about in an overload situation already!"

I would normally have refused to take the assignment because of other demands and pressures on my time. But Ben Alexander is a special person to me. In fact, when he and his family moved to Joplin, Missouri, from Oregon, they lived with our family for six weeks. You get to know someone well when they are living in with you that long. So out of deep respect for Ben, out of trust in his ministry, and out of appreciation for what God can do through one man, I agreed to take the assignment.

But when the manuscript arrived, I neatly tucked it away and, quite honestly, forgot about it. That is totally unlike me. I usually tackle something as soon as I get it in order to work through it and get on to the next project. But I put Ben Alexander's manuscript at the bottom of other projects and then conveniently forgot about it.

One morning as I was leaving for a speaking engagement I remembered the manuscript, picked it up, put it in my bag and took it on the airplane with me. On the airplane I began to read Ben Alexander's book. I could not put it down. This book captivated me. It could have many different titles. It could be entitled, "From the *Sub*-ordinary to the *Extra*ordinary." For this book talks about someone who was born in very sub-ordinary circumstances, but eventually turned his life over to the Lord and the Lord has done the extraordinary through him. The book could be entitled, "From the Unwanted to the Demanded." For this book talks about a man who was not wanted in his early days, but now is in great demand as a counselor, speaker, television and radio guest.

Ben Alexander was born in England and was a functional orphan placed up for adoption immediately after his birth. He grew up in the slum area and was raised by a mother who became a prostitute. When he was fourteen years of age he quit school. Then he bounced around from the military, to taverns, to being a taxicab driver, to being a bakery route man. He experimented with what life meant for him. And that experimentation took him into the pits of hell. During that time he became one of the leading spiritualist activists in London, England. Out of a commitment to that activity he came to the United States for the purpose of spreading spiritualist activity throughout this land.

What Ben Alexander tells you about the activity of the spiritualist, what goes on in a seance, what happens in the secret chambers of a medium, etc. is unbelievable, but is absolutely trustworthy.

I don't believe I have ever met anyone who is as full of integrity as Ben Alexander, nor have I met anyone who is as full of courage as this single man.

Without a high school education and with no college education, he has confronted some of the biggest companies in the United States and through his conversations has caused those companies to change some procedures. A case in point is Sears Roebuck. He has been a special guest on at least fifty radio and television programs per year for the past fifteen years. Ben Alexander has a slogan that he lives by that says this, "What it takes for evil to succeed is for good men to do nothing." So Ben Alexander does something and God touches what he does with His Holy Spirit. Consequently, we can read what God can do through one ordinary person. For instance, recently Ben organized a group of concerned people who literally shut down massage parlors in southwest Missouri.

There is much more to this book than just the activities of a person and the wrongness of the spiritualists, mediums, seances, etc. Read this book carefully and you will discover some of the following powerful influences that can continue to stay alive today in any of our circumstances:

1. The power of a conversation—It was just a superficial conversation of a taxicab driver talking about spiritualism that turned Ben Alexander to that direction. Later, it was a conversation of a customer on a bakery route that began to turn Ben Alexander to the Lord. There is power in our daily conversations. Few of us realize what the long range results will be of the words we say to someone today. We need to be careful with our words.

2. The power of prayer—Carol Huntsinger was just a customer on an ordinary bakery route, but in the heart of this customer, Carol, rose a concern for this delivery man and she never ceased to pray daily that he would become a Christian. She did that for several years without ceasing and the result of that prayer is a Ben Alexander today. Some people claim that prayer really does little good except change the person who is doing the praying, but that is absolutely false! Prayer changes people! Prayer changes things! And, it is time for God's people to tap into the power of prayer!

3. The power of taking a personal interest in someone else's life—A taxicab customer, Ed Engle, began to have an interest in his tour guide, Ben Alexander, and sponsored him to come to the United States. It was out of that personal interest which was backed up by some investment, that God changed Ben Alexander. Isn't it time that we take on more personal interest in someone else's life and take on the responsibility for making their lives different?

4. The power of welcoming a visitor into a worship service—People need to be wanted and to feel a part. Ben Alexander had never been to a worship service in his life until he visited one in the United States. What first of all impressed him was the warm greeting

and acceptance of the people toward a stranger and an outsider. Today the church must learn the power of our first encounter with a visitor to our services on Sunday morning or evening. Is it possible that some people are welcomed more heartily at a supermarket, at a bowling alley, or in a tavern than in our worship services?

5. The power of sharing God's promise of forgiveness—What really struck Ben was a pastor who sat down with him and assured him that God was able and willing and desired to forgive Ben of everything in his past. Ben was drawn to the Lord out of a description of God's grace, not out of a description that God was a celestial attorney ready to pounce on him for his past. People today need to hear the powerful message that God's grace is always greater than man's disgrace.

6. The power of one to one discipling—Ben was taken under the wings of some people who spent time with him on a one to one basis. We do that with our children in our families. And we need to do that with God's children.

7. The power of trusting and helping someone whose background and experiences are different from ours—Ben would never be doing what he is doing now if every Christian he had encountered had shied away from him because his past was so distorted and different from theirs. Many people reached out to Ben because he was now their new brother in Christ and trusted him. Every Christian today needs a Barnabas.

Reading this book can change your life. It can help you to see some of the following:

1. What God can do through an individual who doesn't care who gets the credit.

2. No one needs to stay in the pits that he is presently in.

3. There is hope for anyone.

4. There are certain principles, attitudes and things we can do to help an individual's life to become different. The careful reader needs to spot those and jot them down as they read the various influences that touched this one man's life.

5. The Biblical teachings about spiritualists' activities. As you read this book, jot down all the Biblical references that Ben Alexander mentions. Read carefully the case studies at the end of this book, and you will receive a Biblical education of this topic.

I know of no single man who is more courageous, faithful, open to grow, flexible as Ben Alexander. Although he is well known and in great demand, he is willing to take a telephone call from anyone and spend hours on the phone with that person. He has made himself continually available and accessible. Ben Alexander never meets an unimportant person, nor encounters an unimportant issue in that person's life. He literally pours himself into people and allows people to pour themselves into him.

Few people in this world today allow themselves to be as accessible as Ben Alexander. Ben is interested in service not status.

Reading this book is exciting! But far more exciting is knowing the man about whom this book describes. But what is most exciting is knowing the Christ who has changed Ben Alexander and who uses him.

I am glad Ben Alexander and his family lived with us for six weeks. I rejoice that I know him personally. I am thrilled to relate to him as a friend.

I introduce to you a man who is uneducated from the world's standards but significantly educated from heaven's perspective. Ben Alexander has committed himself to the Word of God and the Word of God to himself. No wonder God has and continues to do so much through one person. And God is willing to do that much through you— if you are also willing.

Knofel Staton

Knofel Staton is president of Pacific Christian College, Fullerton, California. He was formerly a professor at Ozark Bible College, Joplin, Missouri, and Lincoln Christian College, Lincoln, Illinois. He has held ministries in Illinois, Indiana and Iowa.

Staton is a graduate of Lincoln Christian College and has also studied at Illinois State University, Indiana University, Southern Baptist Theological Seminary, Kentucky State, Wheaton Graduate School of Theology and University of Iowa.

He has authored 20 books. He and his wife, Julia, have four children.

SECTION I

AUTOBIOGRAPHY

1

IN THE BEGINNING . . .

I was born on December 25, 1920, in London, England to a widow by the name of Golda Alpern. I was placed up for adoption immediately. In those days it was easy to adopt a child. There were few questions asked. The couple who adopted me barely provided the necessities of life but, still, I am grateful to them for taking me in.

Theft, drunkenness, gambling, prostitution, and bedbugs—all were as common in our part of the East End of London as clean sheets and warm water were in other places. Bookies and prostitutes lived on the street. As children we made money from the bookies by warning them when police were in the vicinity.

My mother, father, brother Morrie (also adopted), and I lived in the last house on a dead-end street called Dura Place. Adjoining the back wall of our house was a stable. All night long we could hear horses kicking against the wall.

We had two rooms, one above the other, about ten feet square each. The first floor served as a kitchen, dining room, living room, and my parents' bedroom. The living area had a small table, some chairs, and a tiny fireplace in which we burned coal or coke. We had no electricity, but only a little gas mantle for light and one gas ring attached to a pipe for cooking.

Because the house was very damp, vermin abounded. In the summertime little white worms crawled all over everything and my body was covered with bedbug bites. One day, in an attempt to kill some of them, I unscrewed one of the bedpost rails and, to my horror, literally hundreds of the bugs came swarming out.

The toilet, which we shared with the family next door, was outside and across the street. It was situated on a sewer and was very dirty. Once when I pulled the chain to flush the water, a sewer rat tried to crawl out. We had no washing facilities in the house. The whole street, which consisted of about ten townhouses, shared one cold-water faucet located outside.

Most of my clothing came from the Jewish Board of Guardians, a welfare organization. On and around High Holy Days, such as Passover, the underprivileged would get matzos, unleavened bread, and all different kinds of food, as well as clothing. The new clothes were exciting because often I would receive a pair of hobnail boots as well. As kids we were delighted to get this kind of boots because we could run behind a horse and cart, hang on to the back rail, and slide along with our boots making sparks from touching the cobblestones.

Sometimes we put our hands into the back of the cart and stole some of the goods. On one occasion, I ran into a deserted building with a stolen package and started unwrapping it. I unwrapped and unwrapped and unwrapped, but there seemed to be no end to the paper. I could see that it was too thin to write on but could not imagine what it was. Of course, later I realized that it was toilet tissue—something I had never seen up to that time.

Every Saturday I was given a penny and a sack-lunch and sent in the public bath. This was a real treat. I often had to wait in line for hours, so I would eat my lunch as I waited. There was always lots of story telling going on between people as they bathed and this kept my attention through the long wait. A towel and a piece of soap were provided at the bath for a penny. There was a man whose job was to clean the bathtubs and run the water. After he cleansed a tub, he would go outside to the faucets and turn the water on. If you gave him a tip, maybe a half-penny, he would give you more hot water. I can still hear people calling out to him through the thin walls saying, "More hot water for number 14," or "More hot water for number 22."

In the evenings I was often given a slice of bread and a penny and sent out for my supper. For the penny I could have chips (fried potatoes) from the fish and chip shop, a baked potato from the potato-vendor, or roasted chestnuts from the chestnut-vendor. All of these vendors and shops were located around a place called Hessel Street which was the Jewish market. There were shops in the buildings, but outside in the street were vendors with all types of food. I was quick with my hands and though the vendors did not know it they provided me with a variety of things to eat.

Morrie, my adopted brother, was about ten years older than I. I do not remember too many happy times with him. He was rather foolish in the things he did and had a sadistic way of playing with me. He would put a pillow over my face and see how long he could stop me from breathing. He was much stronger than I and one night he almost choked me to death.

Morrie and I shared a bed and if I moved in the night and woke him up he would sometimes hit me. One Christmas Eve I had one of my mother's old silk stockings hanging from the bedpost waiting for Santa Claus to come and fill it with toys. I waited up till early in the morning, staring at the fireplace and waiting for Santa to come down. Finally, I fell asleep and the next morning my stocking was stuffed with coal. This was another of Morrie's tricks.

Morrie became a thief and was in and out of prison all the time. When the war broke out, I read in the papers that he had joined the fire department. One day he did not respond to a fire but instead he went through the pockets of all the other firemen. He was taken to court where he was given a choice of prison or going into the armed forces. He chose the air force. The next time I saw him was in a bomb shelter during an air raid. In this shelter there was a crowd gathered around what appeared to be a Royal Air Force officer. It was actually my brother, Morrie, wearing a stolen uniform and bragging about how he had received his ribbons and medals. Later I found out that he had been arrested for impersonating an officer.

Certain conditions at home stand out in my memory. I often read by candlelight. One night I fell asleep while reading. Sometime later I woke up sweating. My bed covers had caught on fire and the bed was burning. The fire had not yet gotten a good start and I was able to smother the flames. Looking back now I realize that I was not nearly as concerned about the fire as I was about my mother's reaction to it. As it turned out, she was just relieved that I was all right.

My father drank heavily, gambled, had affairs, and beat my mother many times. I can still picture my mother with black eyes and swollen lips. She found her life so distressing that she tried to commit suicide a number of times. One evening, after my mother and father had been fighting, she threatened to throw herself out the upstairs window. As she tried to climb out I managed to pull her back. On another occasion I recall her taking the ring off the gas jet and trying to inhale the gas. These were terrifying times for me.

Though my home was not a happy one, I did have good times outside my home. Once a year the Country Holiday Fund sent poor children into the country for a week or so. The first time I went, I was sent to a very pretty place called Sidmouth, in Devon. There, for the first time in my life, I saw a stream. I wondered where it came from and where it was going. Fascinated, I watched the water flow on and on, waiting for it to run out. The following year, at Herne Bay, I first saw a lawn roller. I thought to myself, "What a marvelous machine that would be for pressing pants." So I laid my pants on the ground and proudly pushed the roller back and forth over them.

The bedrooms in the homes where we stayed were lovely. The beds were clean and had real blankets. At home we used coats for covers on the bed. The first home I was taken into had a picture of Jesus on the cross hanging on the wall over my bed. This literally terrified me. I was afraid something evil would happen to me if I slept under the picture.

Near our house was the Boy's Club at Oxford and St. George's. I loved the gymnasium and practically lived there. I would arrive long before anyone else, put down the mats, take out the wooden horse, and practice gymnastics on it. I was pretty good at it and this daily routine of exercise was a great help to me later on in the army.

One of my favorite sports was cricket. Cricket is a sport similar to baseball, but in cricket the ball is "bowled," rather than pitched.

I was a very fast bowler and later became the captain of a cricket team. Soccer was another game I enjoyed. My first pair of soccer boots were second-hand but I was glad to get them. For a soccer ball we would go to the news-vendor, take the old, discarded papers, wrap them into a ball, and tie it up with a string. We thought it was great to have one of these balls and we would play with it for hours.

Boxing was another sport that interested me. While punching a pillow case filled with rags that hung from the clothesline, I would imagine that I was Joe Louis. I did have one actual fight and I did very well until my thumb was dislocated. Then the other fellow punched me all over the place, really battering me. I could not eat for weeks, my jaws hurt so badly. That was my first and my last fight.

Since I could not afford to go to the boxing hall to watch the regular fights, I used to climb up on the roof, go through the skylight over the restroom, and drop down onto the toilet seat. Then I would sneak into the hall, get lost in the crowd, and enjoy the fights for free. The fights often got pretty bloody in those days.

All these things were an important part of my life, but the event that had the single greatest impact on me was the death of my father. I was only eleven years old at the time. The subject of death was considered taboo in our house. It was something to be feared and never talked about. One night as I was lying in my bed upstairs, I could hear my father crying downstairs. He screamed out to God saying, "Please, God, do not let me die! I do not want to die. Please, God help me!"

I will never forget the sound of his crying; it was one of despair, fear, and terror. Now I can understand why he felt that way. He had lived as though he had a thousand years on earth. I will always believe that he knew he was going to Hell, and the prospect of this terrified him.

In the early hours of the morning, his life here ended. I did not sleep that night and in the morning my eyes were red and swollen. As I looked into the mirror, I prayed to God saying, "Please, God, do not let me die," an echo of my father's fears. From then on, the thought of death held a terrible grip on me. I was afraid to sleep at night for fear that I would not be alive in the morning. That fear stayed with me for many years and even now I can still hear my father's screams.

Observing the traditional mourning period for my father, we went to the synagogue every night for a year. We dressed in black, sat on low chairs, and said prayers for him. In those days, a tear was made in your clothing around your heart to indicate that it was torn and broken with grief. This consistent reminder of the man and his death was very frightening to me.

After my Father's death, my mother turned to prostitution to support us. The worst thing was that all the neighborhood kids knew what she did for a living. While we were playing out in the street, everyone could watch the men coming down to see her. This was most embarrassing. I remember one particular man asking me, "Do you know where Fat Annie lives?" Fat Annie was my mother.

This situation contributed much to my low self-image. From time to time, as the money would allow, my mother would make arrangements for me to live in a house down the street or around the block. However, it did not alter what was going on, nor did it change the fact that all my friends knew.

In order to keep me out of the house, mother would provide me with the pennies needed to go to the silent movie. I recall what a trauma it was for us boys when the theater closed for remodelling. The first night it reopened, there was a strong smell of leather seats and paint. The next day in school it was obvious who had been to opening night because we all had a green stripe across the back of our shirts.

My mother read tea leaves and cards. Her friends believed that she was clairvoyant. She picked up feelings from people and gave advice and information to her friends. Though she never involved me in these activities, I was very much aware of them. It was not by chance that as I grew older I was drawn into the occult world.

Our religion, though important to us, was more a tradition than a spiritual commitment. I attended Hebrew School three or four days a week. Of course, the important time for boys comes with the Bar Mitzvah at age thirteen. I spent a long time learning the portion of the Law that I was to speak in the synagogue on my thirteenth birthday.

When the day arrived I was very nervous. And then that morning my mother told me that she had pawned my suit. She drank and smoked a lot and had used the money for cigarettes and beer, I remember standing outside the pawnshop crying because I could not be at the synagogue service for my Bar Mitzvah. I was sure that because of this, I would go to Hell.

For a long time I looked forward to being old enough to quit school and take a job. The law required a child to be fourteen years old before he could do this. When I attempted to quit, there was some difficulty. Apparently, when I was registered in kindergarten, my age was given incorrectly. The school records showed me to be one year younger than I actually was.

Finally, we were able to work things out and I was allowed to quit. I honestly believed that I could help enough with family expenses to allow my mother to stop selling herself. She let me believe that she would stop, but she never did. Her drinking and smoking habits were quite expensive and she never gave them up.

My first attempt to get a job gave me a real taste of anti-Semitism. I was refused the job because I was Jewish. I was told that the firm never closed on Jewish holidays, and even though I insisted that I did not mind working then, I was still turned down.

I did succeed in getting a job in a shoe factory on Brick Lane. I found it difficult to be confined inside for long periods of time, so I did not work there very long. My mother's brother owned a bakery and he hired me for a while. I was allowed to have a loaf of bread each night as a bonus. One night my uncle got upset because the loaf I took cost a penny more than some others, and he fired me.

Other jobs I had included working as a shoe salesman, a packer in a warehouse, and a cutter in the garment industry. On that job we used a large knife and cut about eighty garments at a time.

I also worked on the famous Petticoat Lane selling ties and children's clothes. I even attempted to manufacture a line of children's clothes myself. It was a very small operation and did not last long.

I have jokingly called one job experience my "ten-second job." I had applied for a position at a cement factory and was hired. As I walked in, there was a notice of a collection being taken for a man who had died from inhaling cement dust. For my first assignment, a man threw a heavy bag of cement on my shoulder and told me to carry it across to the other side of the warehouse. By the time I arrived there, my clothes were covered with cement dust and I could barely breathe or see. There was an exit there and I took it, never to return.

Death entered my life again when I was about seventeen. My mother had been in the hospital with bronchial pneumonia, and I had been staying in the house alone. Unfortunately, my mother's "customers" did not know about her illness and constantly came to the door knocking and calling her name. I stayed upstairs in my room, too terrified to move. When Mother died in the hospital, a policeman was sent to the house to tell me. At first, I thought he was just another "customer" and I did not answer the door.

After my Mother's death there was no place for me to go so I stayed in the house. One night shortly thereafter, as I was lying in bed, I could see her standing in front of me at the top of the staircase. She appeared white and etheric-looking and she was smiling at me. It seemed to be some sort of apparition. I put the covers over my head, and when I peeked out, she was gone. It was a terrifying experience and from then on my obsession with death grew worse.

It did not take the landlord long to learn of my mother's death. He sent me a letter asking me to come to see him. He said my mother had owed him back rent and he wanted me to pay it. Until the time of her death, I had given my mother all the money I made and she would give me a small allowance. I did not have a penny to give him. He was a heartless individual and I had to move right away. At the age of seventeen I was completely on my own in the world.

At first this was exciting. But soon I began to get lonely and to feel the need for a close relationship. The Boys' Club was my social life and it was at a dance there that I met a girl named Lily Silver.

Lily and I were immediately attracted to one another and our relationship soon led to marriage. This was in 1940 and a few days after our wedding I was called into the army. During my training and time in the service, Lily stayed with her family.

I was stationed in the Shetland Islands and while there I had an experience that is firmly planted in my memory. It was my job to inspect the soldiers' automatic rifles. This involved looking down into the barrel while each man held his gun, which was of course, empty. I had just stepped back from looking into one gun and still had my hand on it when the fellow pressed the trigger and the gun went off. For me, a matter of two seconds had been the difference between life and death. The incident served to remind me that I was not yet willing or ready to face death.

In May of 1940, I was transferred from the Shetland Islands to mainland England. Here I was given a nine-month course as a wireless radio operator. Wireless operating was a hazardous occupation, as the enemy quickly picked up your signals and you were the first to come under shellfire. We lost many boys that way. But God, in His providence, devised a way to spare me.

My unit was ready for combat duty and prior to embarkation leave we were given two days of sporting events. While high jumping, I injured my ankle and it was very swollen. The following day, a cricket match was held and, despite my injury, I was determined to play because of my love of the game. The position that involved the least movement was that of catcher, which is similar to a baseball catcher behind home plate. (However, in cricket the catcher stands behind a "wicket" and wears no face-mask protector. Also, he wears gloves instead of a mitt, even though a cricket ball is made of cork and leather and is hard like a baseball.)

Unknown to myself or the batter, the pitcher in this game was very fast. He sent a ball flying through the air towards the batter, who had no intention of hitting it. He ducked to avoid the ball hitting him in the face, and instinctively lifted his bat to protect himself.

In the meantime, I had moved to the right to let the ball sail past me, for I had no intention of catching that hard, fast pitch. Unfortunately, or perhaps fortunately, the batter deflected the ball into my face and it hit me straight between the eyes.

I was paralyzed and everyone knew that I had been seriously hurt; some even thought I had been killed. I was taken to a hospital in Leeds, Yorkshire, where I stayed for several weeks. By then, my unit had their embarkation leave and were shipped out to Burma.

It was at about this time that our soldiers were returning from Dunkirk and there were many seriously wounded. As I laid in the hospital with them I listened to them share with one another about their experiences and, of course, sooner or later they asked me about my injuries. The left side of my face was all black and blue, and the blood vessels were severely damaged. I guess I looked to be in worse shape than most. But I simply could not tell them that I had done it on a cricket field, and so I devised all manner of ways to avoid answering.

Visits home were few and far between. Lily and I saw each other about every four or five months. We had no foundation for our marriage and no time to develop one. We were two young people totally unaware of our responsibilities to one another.

By the end of my army career I had become a physical training instructor and thoroughly enjoyed it. I wanted to make it my career, but Lily refused to hear of it. Her father owned a pub and the family insisted that I work in it. I took the job but hated every moment.

The public house business was filthy work and I desperately wanted out. This put a tremendous pressure on my marriage and it began to fall apart. We quarreled constantly. It was during this time that our son, Stewart, was born.

Finally, I left the pub and applied for a job as a London taxi driver. A year of training was required so I got a job in the evenings selling children's clothing.

As part of our training we were given a list of 450 routes to memorize and we rode with a partner until we knew them. We were given monthly exams. Though they lasted only about ten minutes, we had to wait three or four hours to take them. The tests were oral and we never knew what would be asked. The test scores would then be added all together until we reached a certain accumulation of points. Toward the end of our training, the tests changed to every two weeks. At the end of a year I was given a driving exam in a cab and I received my badge.

I was now fully prepared to enter into my new profession. What I was not prepared for was the direction in which I was soon to be led—down streets and alleyways of darkness found on no man's map.

This photo illustrates the typical homes where Ben lived. They were terraced houses and each house contained two rooms.

The bedroom, kitchen, dining room served as the living quarters and was contained in an area 10´×10´. The heat came from the coal fire. There was no electricity and no water. One outside latrine was shared by two houses. There was one cold water faucet for the entire street.

This was the corridor of the bath house. There were no water faucets in the bath itself. An attendant turned the water on from the outside. If you tipped him a ½ penney, he would give you extra hot water. Note handle on right in picture.

This was the Public Bath House that Ben went to once a week. Very few homes had their own bath so the bath houses were used by several hundreds of people in the area. This meant a long wait.

Market scene — this was our shopping mall. You could buy anything from a pin to an elephant.

Much of the transport in those days was horsedrawn. Note the carts filled with hay.

The historic sign of the pawnbrokers is the same as the three golden balls on the coat of arms of the Medici family.

This is the pawnbrokers where Ben's suit was pawned by his mother in the year 1933. Because he did not have a suit, he was unable to be Bar Mitzvahed. Picture shows Ben pointing to the metal bars that once held the golden balls. The shop is now a dress shop.

Ben's old Hebrew school, now a Muslim center — one of our sadder sights.

The Pub where Ben's adoptive parents spent much of their time.

The wall behind Ben is all that remains of the street where he lived as a child.

Ben testifying before the City Council in Joplin, Missouri on June 4, 1985. Inside the box he is holding are pornographic magazines gathered from several of the 52 convenience stores. Over 2,000 people attended the rally at City Hall. Eventually the 52 stores quit selling porn plus two adult bookstores and 6 massage parlors closed.

The Joplin Globe

Joplin, Missouri, June 4, 1985 — Twenty-Two Pages

Vol. 86, No. 304
Copyright © 1985 The Joplin Globe

Anti-porn push packs city hall

By Susan Redden
Globe City Hall Writer

City residents overflowed Joplin City Council chambers Monday night in calling for an ordinance to control pornography.

Council members adopted the ordinance, which had received first-round approval at the May 20 meeting, and city officials promised "vigorous enforcement" of the measure.

Council action came after comments from Ben Alexander, president of the Joplin Chapter of Citizens for Decency Through Law, who called for the city to "send a message to the purveyors of pornography that this noxious material will no longer be tolerated."

His remarks, and those of three others who spoke on the subject, were punctuated with "amens" and applause from members of the huge crowd, described by city officials as the largest ever to attend a council session.

The size of the crowd was difficult to estimate. Its numbers filled the council chambers and municipal building lobby, and overflowed to the steps and sidewalk in front.

"The issue is the moral fiber of our children," Alexander told the council. "Filthy books and magazines and movies that would make the devil blush are being sold in our city. They pervert our children in the sanctity of their homes."

Alexander presented petitions signed by more than 3,800 people and in calling for city action against pornography, which he described as "a cancer that has reached epidemic proportions in our community."

Crowd spills out onto steps and sidewalk at municipal building.

Ben Alexander waves an envelope-clad magazine during presentation.

Globe Photos/GREG SANDERS

SUGGESTIVE PRICE
Daily 75¢ • Sunday 75¢

Louise Gardner, a member of the chapter's committee that monitors materials at adult bookstores and other businesses, said she had been a manager of one of the adult bookstores tell a customer that Joplin "is a good place" for such operations.

"And the biggest tragedy is when adults fill their minds with filth and then exploit children," he said.

Bill Gardner, chaplain with the Jasper County Youth Detention Center, said he is counseling a 12-year-old who is accused of molesting a 4-year-old girl. Gardner said the youth had told him the incident had taken place after he had been exposed to hard-core pornography.

The council also heard from Kathy White, owner of a Joplin child-care center, who described comments she had heard from a child in her care as being "confused" after watching an adult movie rented by her parents.

Alexander told the council he is satisfied with the ordinance, but asked whether its passage would result in enforcement and prosecution of those suspected of violations.

He expressed concern with comments made by City Attorney Michael Talley at the previous council session, when Talley had said the city ordinance permits a statute that has been used law for more than five years and that the city would "look to the county to take the lead in the enforcement effort."

Talley, in comments before and after Alexander's remarks, said it is the intent of local government to "vigorously enforce the ordinance."

"A state statute passed five or six years ago pre-empted the field, and the city had taken the issue into enforcement, and comes within the realm of the county prosecutor," Talley said. "But I understand from your presence here that you are not satisfied with present levels of enforcement."

"Talley's comment, and his promise of enforcement, brought applause from the crowd."

"We had deferred to the county because they, county officials can do so much more in prosecution than the city," Talley said. "We'll still look to them for assistance but we'll no longer defer. We'll enforce the ordinance within the limits of the law and our resources."

He said Police Chief Larry Temus said enforcement efforts are being geared to begin June 24, when the ordinance will go into effect.

This anti-pornography rally was described by city officials as the largest ever to attend a council session.

2

INTO THE DARKNESS

One day in my cab, I picked up an American lady who told me that she was visiting from Oakland, California. She was interested in going to the Spiritualist Association of Great Britain and she began to talk to me about Spiritualism, which was like a religion to her.

As far as I was concerned at that time, religion was all tradition with much ritual and little righteousness to it. Once a year, on the Day of Atonement, I fasted and went to the synagogue to receive forgiveness of sins. My Jewish friends and I generally made an appearance and then left to hold our annual soccer game. We had no commitment to God and there was no abiding happiness in our lives.

Whenever I allowed myself to think about my life, its reason and purpose, I was sure that there was more to it than I had experienced. I conversed with Jehovah's Witnesses and Mormons but found no answers. Church buildings struck me as holy places and I occasionally would go in one to pray. Once I had confessed my sin to God, I felt great. I would leave the church and get into my taxi with a clean feeling inside.

But generally it did not take long for me to begin having and enjoying sinful thoughts again. Why couldn't I stop? Why was there no escape for me? I fully believe that Satan knew I was searching for God and that I was open to suggestion. Before a messenger of truth could come, Satan arranged for one of his servants, a Spiritualist, to fill my need.

The woman in the back of my cab said that she attended seances regularly, and she claimed to have talked with her dead husband through a spirit medium. She spoke of objects rising in the air without being touched by anyone and of a strange thing called a trumpet phenomenon through which she had heard her dead husband's voice. The things she told me seemed incredible.

She then encouraged me to buy a book called *On the Edge of the Etheric.* After reading this book, I became a member of the Spiritualist Association of Great Britain. I soon discovered that they had a library and I read as many books as I could get my hands on. I was hardly able to concentrate on my work. Every available minute was spent at the Spiritualist Association. I went to all the meetings and visited many different Spiritualist churches. Lily did not share any of my interest in Spiritualism.

One Spiritualist in particular fascinated me. His name was Joseph Benjamin and his meetings were always packed. He was a fortune-teller and the things he told people were amazing. It was at one of Benjamin's meetings that I met a family who had a great impact on my life.

Debbie Miller and her sons, Jeff and Michael, talked with me for some time after the meeting. Before we parted they told me that they had a private circle (which is a term for a group of people who meet together regularly to hold seances) and they invited me to come to it. I was thrilled. We soon became close friends and I was a daily visitor.

The developing circle was held on Wednesday. We played with a Ouija board and received messages from it. We would put our fingers on the board and sometimes it would go so fast that one person had to call out the letters while another wrote them down. Most of the time the messages were half-truths and this was confusing.

One phenomenon that consistently took place was a spirit identifying itself to us before we received a message. This was done by the spirit making a sign or spelling its name. There was one spirit, however, that never did this. Instead, we would all feel an uneasy, foreboding presence in the room, and it would become cold. We would feel overshadowed by this spirit and it would spell out a message very deliberately and slowly. The message was always the same: "All is dark. Pray for us."

Sometimes we would do table tapping. After a question was asked, a table upon which we had placed our hands would tap out the number of a letter in the alphabet, spelling out a message. This was a very long process. We also had another table, the top of which was about eight inches square, and it had long legs like a plant stand. Michael would go into a room and choose an object and write it down, not telling us what it was. Then Jeff and I would go in, lay our hands on the table, and ask the table to point out the object. The table would lift off the floor and move quickly to the object in question.

Sometimes through Jeff's mouth we would actually hear the spirits talking to us in voices and we believed that these voices, as well as the messages on the Ouija board and the table tappings, were messages from the dead. Spiritualism had become an unholy fascination for us all.

Eventually, the spirits said, "Look, we are far too advanced to play around with the table and Ouija board. We believe that Jeff, being young and strong, would make a good medium." So Jeff became the medium for the circle.

In reality, he became a substitute savior for the people in our group; we all focused our hopes on him as we sought answers for our individual needs. Jeff was a very strong medium and many different voices would speak through him. We would look at his face and could tell from his expression who would be speaking next. He and I grew to be close friends.

I was anxious to share my new-found religion with my wife but she showed no interest and preferred me not to bother her about Spiritualism. Meanwhile, the rift between us was growing wider.

Then an unexpected opportunity came my way. For years I had dreamed of going to the United States and the chance to make this happen presented itself while I was driving my taxi along a fashionable business street in the West End of London.

I saw a gentleman who was violently shaking leaning against a wall. I jumped out of my taxi to help him. He explained to me that he suffered from Multiple Sclerosis. His name was Ed Engle and he was a successful real estate developer on vacation from Chicago. He requested that I take him to his hotel. When we arrived there he booked me for a sight-seeing tour around the city for the next day.

Ed Engle and I became friends. I invited him to my home for dinner and he met my family. I also chauffered him for the rest of his stay in England. I told him of my desire to live in America and he immediately offered to sponsor my family. My wife was completely against the idea; she did not like the thought of being away from her family.

But I finally persuaded her to go with me to the United States. We sailed on the Queen Elizabeth to New York and then went by train to Los Angeles. Our son, Stewart, was nine years old at the time.

The first place we lived was Whittier, California. I found a job as a bakery route man selling baked goods off the truck. My route was in a suburb called Maywood. This was where I met my first Christian friends, a family by the name of Huntsinger.

Carol Huntsinger was a housewife who came out one day to buy some baked goods from me, or so I thought. (Months later she told me that she had really come out to ask me not to ring the bell that I used to signal to my customers with because it was waking up her child.) Carol saw immediately that I was a Jew and this intrigued her, for she had a burning desire to witness for Jesus to the Jews. She became a regular customer and eventually, Carol and her husband and her child became close friends of mine.

Occasionally, she would speak to me about Jesus, but always in a low-keyed way. She knew that even the mention on the name Jesus upset Lily. Of course, at that time I believed Jesus to be just a good man.

Nevertheless, Jesus was at work in my life through the love and friendship that the Huntsinger family was giving me. No wonder Jesus said, "A new commandment I give to you, that you love one another; even as I have loved you, so you must love one another. By this, all men will know that you are my disciples, if you have love for one another" (John 13:34-35).

Life eventually became unbearable in America. Arguments at home got worse; Lily longed for her mother and became grossly overweight.

I was determined to get a divorce. I cannot help but feel sad to think of the millions all over the world that are even now in the throes of divorce.

A life without Christ is like a ship without a rudder, a ship that goes around and around getting nowhere until it is finally wrecked in a storm. My life and marriage exemplified this.

In December of 1957, we packed and sailed home for England on the Queen Mary. I became a very bitter man. I was secretly planning to leave my wife, but I was concerned about my son. I decided to wait until he turned sixteen before I left home. Looking back, I can see that even this was folly, for I now realize that children need their father no matter what age they are.

Back in England I returned to my taxi driving but I hated it. When I got a fare to Heathrow Airport in London I would wistfully watch the planes leaving for America. I felt cheated and my life was miserable. I became more and more depressed as I saw my dream of returning to America fade. I felt that I was losing out and that one day I would die and that would be the end forever. My obsession with death grew worse.

Upon my return to England, I had tried to get in touch with the Miller family but they had moved and left no forwarding address. There were at least ten million people in and around London at this time and it was a hopeless task to try to find them. Disappointed, I looked for other mediums.

One of these was a Spiritualist medium by the name of Clare Sherrick who lived in the East End of London. She had not known me previously, but when I entered, the first thing she told me was that I had just returned from the United States. I was amazed that she knew this. Then she told me several other things about myself which were true: when I was born, where my mother died, and things of that nature.

While we sat there, strange things began to happen. I could hear rappings coming from a clock. These were spirit rappings. Spirits will take a substance called ectoplasm, sometimes in visible form and sometimes in invisible form, from a person's body and use it for various purposes such as materialization (the actual physical manifestation of a spirit entity) or to move physical objects about.

31

To test the strength of the ectoplasm, they will sometimes rap it against a wall or some other object such as, in this case, a clock. Mrs. Sherrick kept saying to the spirit, "Bless you," and I believed at that point that I was actually contacting the dead.

Mrs. Sherrick left the room and while she was gone I looked at a photo of a little girl. She was about five years old. It seemed as though the girl in the photo spoke to me and told me, "That's my Mummy. I am Rebecca of Sunnybrook Farm." She kept laughing and repeating herself, "I am Rebecca of Sunnybrook Farm."

The medium came back into the room and immediately sensed that something was happening. I will never forget her saying to me, "Come on, give . . . give!" She wanted me to tell her what I was experiencing. I did and she said, "Ah, bless her little heart, that is my little Becky. She was killed outside this house here by a lorry (truck)."

Now I was absolutely obsessed with Spiritualism. I spoke of it to every customer I picked up who would listen to me. There was a weekly newspaper called the "Psychic News" and I could hardly wait for it to come off the presses so that I could read it. I was truly hooked.

One day, while driving my taxi in Stoke Newington, I came round a curve in the road and saw my old friend's mother, Mrs. Miller, just going into a grocery store. Had I been a couple of seconds later I would have missed her. I sounded my horn and caught her attention. She ran over to the taxi, apparently as delighted to see me as I was to see her.

She said, "Ben, you know, the guides kept saying we were going to meet again." She was speaking of spirit guides. These were certain spirits who consistently manifested themselves through a particular medium, such as Jeff, to oversee or direct the psychic phenomena that occurred during a seance.

I was amazed—not only to meet her six miles away from where they had once lived, but also to hear that the spirits had foretold that we would meet again. Then she said, "Guess what? Jeff has gotten materialization!" I could hardly believe my ears. Ever since I had become interested in Spiritualism I had been hoping to see this phenomenon of the solidification of spirits.

I was really excited. We drove to her place and found Jeff at home. He appeared happy to see me again. He told me, "Ben, I do not know what is going on. I go upstairs in the seance room and go into a trance. While I am in a trance state Mike takes pictures.'' He then proceeded to show me photos of spirits that had literally solidified.

Jeff said the pictures had been taken in an upstairs seance room so I asked to go look at the room alone. I told Jeff that I wanted to pray but I really wanted to check the room for trap doors and such.

The room was sparsely decorated. It contained a curtained chair, a large, old family Bible, and a number of chairs for participants in the seance. On the walls were pictures that Jeff had painted of spirit guides, including one in particular who called himself ''Mr. Richards.'' This spirit claimed to be a reincarnated Pharaoh, and the face portrayed in Jeff's painting was that of a cold, cruel-looking man.

Also on the wall was a cross. The presence of the Bible and the cross was not unusual. In seances we always prayed over the Bible to Jesus, since he was considered to be a medium of the highest order.

I returned downstairs and visited with Jeff for a while. I was thrilled. This was a Saturday sometime in 1958 and was the beginning of six years of fascinating experiences in the seance room. I had been searching so long and felt that this was another step that would lead me in my quest for the truth about life after death.

At last the time for the seance arrived. Around 6:30 the sitters began coming in. I could hardly contain myself I was so excited. Jeff went in first, and then his brother Mike, his mother, his Aunt Rose, and a widower named Joe Coleman. Then Jeff's cousin Jack went in with his wife, and finally, it was my turn.

Jeff sat in the chair behind the curtain. The lights were turned off except for a red light. It was very dark but our eyes became accustomed to it and we were able to see one another in the red glow. Someone prayed over the Bible and asked Jesus to favor us with psychic phenomena. Then a phonograph was turned on. Music seems to be necessary, for without sound the phenomena will not take place.

The Bible tells us in Revelation 16:14 that demons would work miracles in the last days. We were about to see this but I did not realize it. The air in the room suddenly grew cold and someone said the conditions were good for the spirits to contact us. We sat there with our hands held out, palms up, as this is supposed to be the source of the energy force that goes towards the medium.

There was an air of expectancy. Suddenly, the curtain around Jeff opened just a little and a strange face showed itself. I will never forget that face. It was very white and etheric-looking. It certainly was not Jeff's face. When I saw it I prayed in my heart, "God, thank you, thank you for showing me life after death." I was ecstatic; my dream had come true. I had heard about other people's experiences but had never before seen this kind of thing myself.

The curtain parted and the spirit stepped out. It looked like a person from the ancient past. It had on a white robe, of the type that people wear in Eastern countries, and a turban around its head. Around the legs were something that looked like graveyard wrappings.

The spirit walked out into the room. Attached to it was a long piece of white ribbon or rope formed from ectoplasm which stretched back under the curtain. The spirit walked to me and looking at me said in a deep Scottish accent that they welcomed me and were glad to have me be there; that I would give extra added power to the circle.

I said, "May I shake your hand, please?" The spirit replied, "Yes, in a moment, in our own time." It then stepped back and a strange thing happened. The form in front of me began to sink through the floor. First the legs disappeared, then the trunk, and lastly, the neck and head. The white ribbon then went back under the curtain and obviously into Jeff's stomach. It was all fascinating and I was thrilled.

Then something happened. The light went out and I heard a voice. It said, "Benjamin, we would like to shake hands with you now. Please extend your hand forward." It was totally dark in the room. I had an eerie feeling as I put my hand out. The hand that gripped mine was no ordinary hand but was covered with some kind of fur. I nearly died with fright! I am amazed that I did not have a heart attack. Satan loves the dark and he loves fear.

The spirits explained to me that they were testing me to see if I could stand up to shocks. They said that they were working on a scientific experiment and needed the right type of person. That, of course, turned out to be a lot of nonsense.

After this experience I began to get used to the phenomena and it did not frighten me as much. Satan knew how badly I wanted to know about life after death and he really had me spellbound. I was like a person who takes heroin into his body. He knows it can kill him but still he cannot stop.

We had a schedule of regular activities. On Wednesday nights we had a developing circle with an experienced medium in charge. There were soft lights and soothing music, and people were encouraged to go into trance. Very often psychic phenomena took place. Occasionally, someone would give a prophecy. Hands were laid on the sick and tongues were spoken. Spiritualists claim these things to be the gifts of the Holy Spirit.

Phenomena became a regular occurrence in our developing circles. Often Joe Coleman would go into trance. His face would transform and he would look like an Indian. Jeff, too, would sometimes look like an Indian and the two would begin speaking to one another in what we assumed was an Indian language. As abruptly as they began, they would stop talking. One of them would begin beating the table like a tom-tom and the other would dance around. This was supposedly the spirits of Indians reliving their life on earth.

On one occasion at a seance, Mr. Richards, the controlling spirit guide of Jeff Miller, folded his legs as he usually did and said, "Benjamin, I want to remind you of a statement you made several months ago." Then he beckoned with his fingers for someone to bring something to him. We could not see anyone or anything but he seemed to be flipping through pages with his fingers as though he had a file in his hand. He then began to read something which I had said about six months earlier. The startling thing was that it was exactly as though I was listening to a tape recording that I had made a long time ago. It was most uncanny and, of course, fascinating. Imagine Satan keeping books!

Knowing of my experience in the United States, the spirits made it clear that they hated America. At the time I did not understand why, but now that I think back on it, the reason becomes clear. The spirits advocated communism. I heard them talking about it during several discussions we had. That certainly goes along with Satan and his ways because communism is atheistic and anti-Christ.

We not only worked in Jeff's home during these so-called experiments but we also went to Joe Coleman's home. The same type of phenomena took place. As ususal, Mr. Richards acted as the chief spirit in control of everything. He was also chief doorkeeper. One time he announced, "Aunt Rose must go! Her services are no longer required. She is an ectoplasmic parasite."

During a seance, ectoplasm comes out in an invisible form from the sitters and is drawn to the medium to be used by the spirits to produce their phenomena. This was being drained off by Aunt Rose. She suffered from tuberculosis and instead of giving off ectoplasm. She was drawing it to herself for healing.

The spirits felt that Aunt Rose's weakness was affecting the phenomena. We had to tell her and it was a bitter blow to her. Spiritualism was her life, as it was for all of us. In my case, it was giving me proof of life after death and taking my fear away. Joe Coleman lived in hope of one day speaking to his dead wife. Mrs. Miller hoped to contact her deceased husband, and likewise, Michael Miller wished to reach his dad.

Many strange things took place in the seance room. Often it would feel cold to us. I later learned that this was because ectoplasm was being taken from us in order for the spirits to solidify. Satan uses a life force that God has given us to work his counterfeit signs and wonders.

On one particular occasion the room was in total darkness; it was just impossible for us to see anything or anybody. A voice said to me, "Are you cold, Benjamin?" I was shivering but how the spirit could have seen me in such darkness I don't know. The voice continued, "We shall soon take care of your cold," and suddenly something dropped on my head.

I almost died with fright! The lights came on and I found myself covered with a wool-lined coat—a coat that had been left downstairs in another room! The door in the seance room was locked; the coat had been teleported.

Other things not originally in the room would find their way in during a seance. It was eerie and sometimes even frightening, but still very fascinating. The Bible tells us in II Thessalonians 2:9-11 that "The coming of the lawless one will be in accordance with the work of Satan displayed in all kinds of counterfeit miracles, signs, and wonders, and in every sort of evil that deceives those who are perishing. They perish because they refuse to love the truth and so be saved. For this reason God sends them a powerful delusion so that they will believe the lie." Satan truly had us believing his lies and firmly in his grip.

There was one thing that happened rather often and always disturbed me. We always had a Bible in the room. Frequently it would rise off the table in the red light with no one touching it. The Bible would then fly through the air and smash against the wall. One time a materialized spirit picked it up, peered into it very closely, and then threw it clear across the room. Since I believed that we were doing God's will, this was hard to understand. Whenever this happened the spirits would say that an evil spirit had gotten through and that it would not happen again. But it continued.

As time went by, the things taking place in the seance room began to take on a different nature. I noticed that the materialized spirits were becoming more terrifying and ugly. These entities looked very evil; they were very bad and very frightening.

One Wednesday night Mr. Richards said, "We are going to bring in a Linga-Sierra on Saturday." When I asked what that was he just said, "You will find out, Benjamin, on Saturday." I continued, "Where does it come from? What is it? Who is it?" He replied, "Oh, we will be bringing one from a nearby graveyard." Then he said, "And what's more, we plan to dematerialize the cross you are so fond of sitting under." I always sat under the cross because I felt protected.

Evil began to fill the room and I felt hysterical inside. Somehow I managed to stay until the seance was over. We always took notes and this particular time we had a discussion about what a Linga-Sierra might be. We had read many books on Spiritualism but none of us knew what this entity was.

The next day I hurried to the library at the Spiritualist Association of Great Britain. Some of the most educated mediums in the country were there and I asked them if they had ever heard of the Linga-Sierra. None of them had. I then spoke to a friend of mine who was a secretary at the Association. Her name was Miranda. She suggested that I go to the Theosophical Society. This was a group that accepted every religion in the world, including Spiritualism.

The library at the Theosophical Society did have a book on the Linga-Sierra. The book indicated that it was a spirit that chose to linger around the remains of its former physical body.

On Saturday night the promise of the Linga-Sierra appearing was fulfilled. In the seance room there was no light but we could hear a type of sobbing. It was eerie and terrifying. I have two photographs taken in the seance room of the Linga-Sierra and they show a most horrifying face. People have asked why Satan would allow those pictures to be taken. I feel that he had nothing to lose. To the Christian who doubts the presence of Satan's power in this world the pictures mean nothing.

I was not the only one to witness this; the others in the room saw the same thing. It amazed me that Satan knew about the Linga-Sierra. No one in the seance room, including Jeff, had ever heard of such a thing. It was not until I went to the Theosophical Society that we learned about it. The vast realm of Satan's knowledge is disturbing.

On one occasion Mr. Richards suggested an experiment to see if a materialized spirit could stand a stronger light. I was all for that—I had had enough of darkness! But I certainly did not expect what happened next.

The spirit told me that at a given moment I was to turn on the flashlight. When I turned on the light we could see the ectoplasm pouring out of Jeff. It then shrank back so fast it sounded like a shotgun. It looked like a huge piece of elastic flying back into Jeff's stomach.

Jeff screamed and fell from the chair, landing face down on the floor. Quickly, we turned on the lights in the room and found Jeff lying in a pool of water. Ectoplasm, just like the rest of the physical components of our bodies, is composed mostly of water. The sudden return of the ectoplasm from solid to liquid state as it tried to re-enter Jeff's body caused this watery residue. Jeff's stomach had a six or eight inch blood-red circle on it, as if it were in hemorrhage.

We carried Jeff downstairs. We thought he was going to die. He was groaning in pain. It needs to be noted here that while we were very concerned about Jeff, we also wanted to keep the phenomena coming. It was very important to all of us—even more important than Jeff's health.

After a while Jeff recovered enough to eat some sandwiches. As he ate, he began going into trance. However, a different spirit spoke through him this time saying, "We are not going to have any more problems after this. I am coming back." We recognized this spirit to be "White Owl," a spirit guide that had controlled Jeff before we had the phenomenon of materialization and before Mr. Richards had appeared. He really seemed rather gentle when compared to Mr. Richards, the so-called reincarnated Pharaoh. White Owl spoke again saying, "In the future I will be in charge."

The following Saturday Jeff sat again. We waited as he went into a trance, fully expecting to hear White Owl's voice. My heart sank as Mr. Richards' sinister voice came through demanding, "What is this nonsense about this White Owl being in charge? I am still in command here!" Mr. Richards went on to say, "I have a surprise for you."

Ectoplasm began to come out of Jeff, pouring into the room, and a spirit built up. When the spirit spoke we all recognized the voice as belonging to Jeff's father, Mike Miller. The spirit looked at Mrs. Miller and said, "Debbie," in the same deep voice we all knew. Mr. Miller had smoked heavily when he was alive and it had affected his lungs and throat.

Mrs. Miller answered, "Ike, Ike," and began sobbing. The spirit walked over to her and she stood up and embraced it. She continued to cry and sob. Then he sat her down and turned to his son. He said, "Michael." The same thing happened. Mike stood up, held his dad, and cried.

Then he turned to me. Now I was actually seeing these things. I had helped to pull the ectoplasm from my friend's stomach but I could hardly believe all of this—even when I knew it was fact. This was really happening. I could see this man with my own eyes; I could hear his voice.

He looked at me and said, "How are you, Ben?" I said, "I am fine, Mr. Miller." I was trying to peer closely because, although we had a red light in the room, it was still dark and difficult to see.

Then something really staggering happened. He stepped back and said in a deep voice, "I am going to get in trouble; I don't care. I am going to get in trouble; I don't care." He kept saying these words over and over and his body began sinking through the floor—first the feet, then the trunk—and he said, "Stop this! You're killing my boy! Stop this! You are killing my boy!" And the voice trailed off weaker and weaker and with the final "Stop this! You are killing my boy," the ectoplasm went back into Jeff's stomach.

I have always been puzzled by this. I do not know if the spirit, Mr. Miller, was concerned about his boy, or if it was Satan with another of his lying signs and wonders trying to convince us beyond a shadow of a doubt that it was real. Satan fully knew that none of us would stop this kind of thing.

It seemed as if the seances were going from bad to worse. The spirits, as always, speaking through Jeff, were telling us that they wanted to bring entities from different planets. Their reason for this was to convince scientists of their existence.

Frankly, I thought this was ridiculous. But I was afraid to speak up. I was terrified that they would kick me out, for at one time they had wanted to do this.

Other accidents also occurred causing Jeff to bleed from the nose or mouth. Spiritism is very dangerous and mediums have been known to lose their lives through this phenomenon. Ectoplasm is a life force and Satan uses this energy to clothe demon spirit entities. The very life force is taken from a person. Satan cannot create but he can take things from a body and make something from it. He attempts to counterfeit God by producing demons in solid form. This was not trickery or fraud.

The creatures we saw were horrible, ugly monstrosities. One was supposedly half-human and half-gorilla. I feel strange even talking about it because it was so incredible, so unbelievable. Spiritism is a horrid and frightening thing.

The lights were turned out and it was very dark. Though we could not see anything, we could hear this creature. It would grunt, "Ungh, ungh," in a deep croaking sound. It was weird and quite terrifying. But we could never see anything. We could hear footsteps as it walked around the room.

Then it did something very strange, a foolish little thing. It would go to a man and grovel at his feet, taking off his shoes and undoing the laces, saying, "ungh, ungh, ungh," as if it was enjoying doing this. I remember because it did this to me often. Then it would exchange shoes, putting the ladies' shoes by a man and a man's shoes by a woman. Then it would grunt some more. I thought to myself, "How foolish!"

Some of the people would laugh. I felt that the laughter was probably to relieve their fear. Eventually, the spirit seemed to zero in on this fear and wanted us to see the creature. The grunts became louder and the footsteps heavier. The red light was turned on and we were able to see this thing.

It was simply horrible! All we could see at the time was a turban around its head and thick fur on its face, and its grotesque lips and big teeth. I have in my possession a photo of this, but people think it is not a real picture and I do not blame them. I saw it for myself and still find it difficult to believe. But these things are very real.

Then the creature began to pick up the sitters and carry them around the room. This was supposed to be funny, but I was getting more and more terrified as this continued to take place. Then the spirits decided on another type of phenomena. They said that there were animals crawling around us. I never saw these but I could feel something crawling about my legs.

Other things were taking place, too. It seemed that each seance got more and more fearful. Yet, I kept going. I do not know why. I was always frightened when I went, and I felt that I wanted to run away from it. I guess the obsession of wanting to know about life after death stopped me from leaving this circle of fear.

One time during a seance, I felt something behind me. I was not sure what it was but I turned my head and I got a shock. Behind me was a mummy. I literally saw a mummy! It was bandaged from head to foot. Now I do not remember exactly how long we had been in the seance room, but the lines of the bandages on this mummy were so perfect, it would have taken hours to create one fraudulently.

It seemed ridiculous! I was seeing these things but I could not believe them. Many people say to me, "Ben, I believe you, but you were probably hypnotized." I was not hypnotized. We were allowed to take photographs of these things at certain times and I tell you, you cannot hypnotize a negative. No, they were real!

Now I was the only one who turned around to see this thing; no one else knew of the mummy. I happened to be holding Mrs. Miller's hand in the circle so I pulled on it and as she turned around and saw this entity, she screamed in fear. I looked at this stupid thing and not knowing what to say I said, "Bless you, brother." Eventually, it started going through the floor and the ectoplasm went back into the spirit medium as it always did.

As time went on, things went from bad to worse. The last seance I was involved in with Jeff Miller was too much for me. It related to his cousin. This poor woman went to pieces and became hysterical and screamed with fear. No doubt, she never returned and neither did I.

About two weeks later, I came down from my apartment to go to work. My taxi was parked in the street and as I opened the door I froze and broke out into a cold sweat. There was a white envelope laying on the driver's seat. I opened it, trembling with fear, for I knew where it had come from. It was a message from the spirits in the seance room that had been dictated and delivered to me. As I remember, it said, "We will deal with you when we get you over the other side." Obviously, the spirits were upset that I was not showing up for the seances.

I was simply trembling with fear and I went straight to the Spiritualist Association. I showed it to Miranda, the woman who had helped me before, for we had become close friends. She in turn showed it to the Secretary of the Association, the late Ralph Rossiter.

He told me that ours was an evil circle and that I should come out of it. I said, "Look, we prayed to Jesus. We asked for good spirits." He said, "No, obviously this is an evil circle."

I received more letters in the same fashion in my taxi. I wish now that I would have kept them, but I destroyed them. I felt that was best. Satan, through Spiritualism, had built up a fear syndrome in my life and I was terrified. I lived in fear and uncertainty, not knowing what to do. I was absolutely beside myself with fear.

Eventually, Miranda suggested that I start my own circle. We began to hold seances with her mother, her sister and a cousin of theirs. I also began sitting on my own and soon began to get rappings in the room. I will never forget the first rappings, they were so clear. I was frightened but I was also excited because I thought, "I am getting the power now. I am going to be a physical spirit medium." There is no doubt in my mind that when Satan said to Eve, "Ye shall be as gods," Eve wanted something that would make her above others, that would give her knowledge of a higher kind. This wanting to know the beyond is a mystic experience which people really look for. And I was looking for this, too.

Miranda did not want me to do physical phenomena such as rapping and materializing because she knew the harm it could cause to a medium's body. I knew, too, but the idea of being used as a medium and of people coming to see me was attractive. This, of course, was nothing more than pride and that is the way Satan works; that is the way people fall–through pride.

Meanwhile, things at home gradually went from bad to worse. Finally, my marriage broke up. Eventually, I divorced Lily and married Miranda.

The saddest part of all is that my son, Stewart, became the victim of incompatible parents. We occasionally met secretly in a park in North London. One particular meeting still haunts my mind. It was the last one I had in December 1964 when I decided to return to America. I could hardly find the heart or courage to tell him. As we sat the bench, we had little, if anything, to say to each other. My heart is still sad as I remember, most vividly, the large tears falling from my son's eyes and dropping into the sand at our feet.

But Miranda and I had our minds made up, and with our hopes set on a brighter future, we left for America. The "brightness" we sought would indeed come to us, but from a source that we never suspected.

3

INTO THE LIGHT

When I arrived in America my soul was tormented. I felt like a fugitive. Fear of death, hopelessness, and guilt seemed to be my lot. I did not want to die because I believed I was destined for Hell. I did not want to live because of unbearable guilt. I felt guilty about the break-up of my marriage.

Even though Spiritualism taught me that there was no such thing as Hell, my Jewish teachings about breaking the Ten Commandments haunted me. I believed that God would punish me. The Bible says in Galatians 6:7, "Be not deceived; God is not mocked, for whatsoever a man sows, that shall he also reap."

I was sending home support to Lily. In return I received abusive letters, and she absolutely refused to allow any communication to pass between my son and me.

After I had been in America for several weeks, I finally got a job for a bakery company by the name of Helms. I decided it was time to visit the Huntsinger family again. I wondered how they would feel toward me after I told them of the collapse of my marriage. We drove to Norwalk from Santa Monica, where we were living at the time. The Huntsingers were just delighted to see me and to meet Miranda. Carol said that she finally expected this to happen, especially the way our marriage had been going. I then proceeded to tell Carol what our plans were, that Miranda was a Spiritualist who had worked as a secretary for the Spiritualist Association in Great Britain, and that I was a practicing medium.

I was excited with the prospects of opening up a Spiritualist organization in this country and I expected her to be thrilled about this. Sometime later, she told me that she had been heartbroken as she listened to me.

I asked her about her church and said that I would like to go there and meet the people. The purpose of my going to the church was twofold: first, I wanted to meet some nice people and socialize; and secondly, I wanted to convert them to Spiritualism. I felt so sure that I had the truth. Little did I realize that this was going to be a turning point in my life, and that a surprise awaited me.

I guess you might say that the seeds of Christianity had been sown in my life during the first year I had lived in the United States, in the year 1956-57, due to the love and kindness of the Huntsinger family. Now those seeds were about to take root.

It was a long drive from Santa Monica to Norwalk on Sunday, February 14, 1965, but it turned out to be the most important day of my life. I sat in the service and listened to the minister, whose name was Reverend Orrin Kingsriter. This was the first time that I had ever actually attended a worship service.

I distinctly remember the minister preaching from the Old Testament. He knew that I was Jewish, and I believe that in his wisdom and God's guidance he chose to do this for my benefit. He read from Isaiah 1:18 and the words still ring in my ears today. He said, "Come, now and let us reason together,' says the Lord. 'Though your sins are as scarlet they will be as white as snow; though they are red like crimson, they will be like wool.'"

I thought about the words he spoke: "Though my sins are as scarlet, they will be made as white as snow." What a wonderful thought. Those are the words I can remember the minister preaching. But the thing that really struck me was that when the service was over, the people came over to me and welcomed me warmly. They shook my hand and seemed genuinely pleased to see me.

I had never had anything like this happen to me in my life. Never before had people been concerned about me and so, naturally, I was a very, very happy man. I was invited to come back again in the evening and though it was a long way from where we lived, Miranda consented to do so.

During the evening service, the church held a "singspiration." This again was something new to me. People were clapping, praising the Lord, and singing songs. I remember seeing the minister walking up and down the aisle singing along with the music. And then something got hold of me. I arose out of my seat and said to him, "Pastor, I would like to be with your people. I would like to belong to your church." He invited me to go into his office.

When in his office, he said to me, "Ben, would you like to pray with me?" I had not gotten down on my knees in years. (Well, I had, actually, on my own, but not with somebody else being there.) However, I got on my knees, and he started praying to God and talking to me about Jesus.

Then he explained to me how God forgives us of everything we have done in our lives, and he began to point out scriptures that stated this. I said, "Pastor, this is impossible. Nobody could forgive me for what I have done." He read from I John 1:9, "If we confess our sins, he is faithful and righteous to forgive us our sins, and to cleanse us from all unrighteousness." He made me read it through several times, and I kept saying to him, "No, not for what I have done."

"All of us believe that our sins are the worst," he said. Then he made me read I John 1:9 again and especially the words, "to cleanse us from all unrighteousness." I have since learned that I John 1:9 was actually written to Christians, but at that time I did not know that. Just the very fact and the very thought of forgiveness was overwhelming to me.

Then Reverend Kingsriter asked me if I would believe that Jesus was the Messiah. At that time I knew very little of the Scriptures, but I was in such a state, I would have believed in anybody if I knew there was forgiveness. And so I did accept Jesus as my savior and I was a very, very happy man. As I went home with Miranda, the feeling of being forgiven was just tremendous; it was a wonderful experience. Of course, we know our faith does not come by feelings— "Faith cometh by hearing and hearing the word of God" (Rom. 10:17). Nevertheless, I was exuberant.

The following day I went to work feeling happy and I told my customers that I had been saved. That evening Miranda and I sat down to hold a seance. I went into a trance and spirits began to speak through me to her about my new-found religion, Christianity. They said this was fine and that they felt it was just great. Then they said another spirit would like to come and take over and speak through me, and as Miranda later told me something very strange happened.

Suddenly, a new personality began to sing hymns through me. But right in the middle of a hymn, I just threw my hands up, came out of the trance, and said, "I do not want to do this anymore." I said, "We need to move to Norwalk and we need to be near those people now." I really did not know why I was saying this, but I now believe it was the leading of the Holy Spirit. And so we just packed everything up and moved to Norwalk, California, to be next to the church.

Arrangements were made for us to stay with a family for a few days in their guest house. Carol had given me a Bible and while I was in this home I began to read it. In fact, it was the first time that I had really looked into the Bible. I had prayed over it many times as a Spiritualist but I had never read it.

And I really believe that it was the providence of God that led me to the eighteenth chapter of Deuteronomy. I opened up the Word and I was shocked as I read about Moses warning the Children of Israel as they were about to enter the Promised Land, that they must not follow after the ways of the Caananites. Moses said, "When you enter the land which the Lord your God gives you, you shall not learn to imitate the detestable things of those nations. There shall not be found among you anyone who makes his son or daughter pass through the fire, one who uses divination, one who practices witchcraft, or one who interprets omens, or a sorcerer, or one who casts spell, or a medium, or a spiritualist, or one who calls up the dead; for whoever does these things is detestable to the Lord and because or these detestable things, the Lord your God will drive them out before you" (Deut. 18:9-12).

I was shocked at what I was reading because we had been doing the very things which were disgusting in the eyes of God. Then I began to look at the concordance and I was amazed as I went through the Scriptures to find well over 100 verses that condemned these things that we thought were of God. This certainly was a new understanding, but it was not difficult for me to realize how true the Bible was, especially after the experiences I had had in Spiritualism.

Three days later, on Wednesday, February 17, I received a telephone call from Reverend Kingsriter. He said he wanted to speak to me about something important. I went to see him at his office and he said to me, "Ben, now that you are a Christian there is a second blessing for you, the baptism of the Holy Spirit."

He showed me several scriptures in the Bible that he felt referred to this, and after reading them, he encouraged me to speak in tongues, which I did. I practiced speaking in tongues for four and a half years but eventually gave this practice up as I felt more comfortable praying in my own language.

Meanwhile, my friend, Carol Huntsinger, had helped me to get work at a company called Reliance Dairies. At that time the owner was a man named Demos Shakarian. His son, Richard, was the vice-president and a man by the name of Howard Jones was the manager. I managed to land a job as an advertising salesman, and Howard Jones and I became close friends. Later on, Reliance Dairies went bankrupt and I went into the insurance business.

It was about that time that our daughter, Mary, was born to us. We were very excited, just thrilled! I can remember Dr. Charney at the hospital in La Mirada coming over to me and telling me that I was the father of a little girl who had ten fingers and ten toes. I remember picking up Dr. Charney and twirling him around and around and around.

We were living in an apartment complex where there was a swimming pool, and they allowed us to stay there for six months, but then we had to move out. By that time I had saved money and we put a down-payment on a small house in Norwalk.

I was very zealous as a Christian and would witness wherever possible. I was happy meeting lots of new Christian friends, but despite my happiness, many times I would think of my past life. It seemed as though I could never get my son, Stewart, out of my mind.

Sin is like a cancer. Even when you have repented and been forgiven, it seems that you are always reminded of it. A man who has cancer in his chest goes to a surgeon who takes out the cancer, cleans the man, completes a successful operation, and then sews the man back up. But the scars on his chest will always remind him that he once had the cancer. And the scars of my sins always remind me of what I once had been. But, praise God, I know that I am now redeemed.

After a while, Miranda and I became rather disenchanted with California. We thought it was too much of a rat-race. Nor was I very happy in my job as an insurance man. So in September of 1969 we decided to move. Mary was about two and a half years old at the time. We were sorry to go, but everything was packed and the new move took place as we went north to Grants Pass, Oregon.

Here, I believe, was another turn for the better in my life as a Christian. I immediately made my acquaintance with an Assembly of God Church and met a Dutch family who were kind enough to help us by storing our furniture.

Meanwhile, I found a pretty little house. Miranda and I loved it, and these people helped us move in. I got a job selling for Fuller Brush. It was not easy; our life was very hard there and I was soon getting behind on the rent.

About this time, I visited another church. I met the minister there and told him my story. He said he had just bought a house and had turned it into a nursing home for elderly men. He asked if Miranda and I would take on the job of managing the home. He would pay me a salary and would give us free board and lodging. We felt that this was definitely of the Lord.

So, we moved into this new place with our little Mary, who was about three years old at the time. My job was to be the caretaker. I did a lot of painting, cleaned the rooms, took care of the elderly people, and served the meals Miranda cooked.

But after the first few weeks, we were not paid any money and I was disturbed about this. The minister then told us that he could not afford to pay us. Although this was upsetting, I felt that at least we still had food and lodging. But then we had another shock. He said the place was not really paying for itself. So he suggested that Miranda and I go and apply for food stamps because he was unable to give us any food.

Things were going from bad to worse and we felt trapped. We did not know what to do. We still had some bills to pay from a loan we had taken some time ago. Then this minister, whom we had begun hearing many sad stories about, said he was no longer going to look after old people. He planned to get rid of them and he was going to get money from the Government to house delinquent teenagers. We were very unhappy about this as we did not want our child to be exposed to this type of environment.

Well, it all turned out to be a blessing in disguise for when the authorities investigated this man they found him to be unsuitable. They then approached us and explained that they had also investigated us and found nothing on our record. They could not understand why we were mixed up with this man, so we explained our circumstances. We were then offered help. They would be able to give us a grant through welfare because we had a child, and they would help us get on our feet.

They gave us an allowance so we were able to move and we found the cheapest place we could. It was a converted cowbarn and it was not very pleasant, but at least it took us away from the environment we had been in. They were even going to help me through college. I took an entry test, passed, and was accepted at the college in Medford, Oregon. I was to study to become a school teacher. But unfortunately, the Government funds were dropped and I was unable to follow through with this.

While all this was happening, my church life had changed. I had met a family south of Grants Pass at a Pentecostal church. I was still a member of the Pentecostal faith and this family invited me to become a member of their church. Their particular congregation was the family, itself. There was a widowed lady and her three daughters and two sons. The eldest daughter was adopted and she was the minister.

51

These people were very poor, they lived on a small acreage, grew their own food, kept rabbits, chickens, and goats. They were very kind and shared their food with us. We will forever be grateful to them.

We often visited other churches and I remember that we were getting rather disenchanted with the way things were going. The more I read the Bible about the gifts of the Holy Spirit, the more confused I became, to be frank with you, I was not seeing the miracles taking place in these churches that we were visiting. It seemed that Miranda and I were becoming more and more disillusioned with our religion.

Before leaving for a church we would pray God would lead us to the right church. I still believe at that time in our lives we were looking for signs and wonders, not realizing that Jesus said, "only an evil and adulterous generation seeks after a sign" (Matt. 12:39).

One particular church we went to was called the Metropolitan Tabernacle in Grants Pass Oregon. We had a rather distressing experience. The service started with a victory march. The minister instructed the first row to get up and started marching around the aisles in the church, then the second row and so on. The people would all be marching around the church, clapping their hands and singing "Victory in Jesus." Miranda and I sat in the back row and did not move. Everyone looked at us as though we were heathens. So in embarrassment we finally joined in marching around the church.

We were then told to form a circle and lift our hands and pray to God. The minister was obviously pleased and pointed to me and told the congregation that God had told him that the shekina glory was on my face, just like it was on the face of Moses (Exod. 34:29-35).

I was happy with what I felt was a sign and prophecy from God. But it was short lived. The visiting evangelist stopped the minister, saying "nonsense this man is not from God, but is demon possessed."

I was stunned and shaken. My spirit was crushed. The congregation was told to return to their seats. The evangelist then gave his sermon. Later he called on people with problems and began to cast demons out of them.

After the service, Miranda and I went to speak to him privately. He was in the office with the minister, to whom I said, "Now look, something is wrong here. You told me I had the glory of God upon my face, "and to the visiting evangelist I said "You, sir, said I was demon possessed. Now one of you is wrong.'' The minister said, ''Just a moment, the Lord is speaking to me,'' he then continued, ''I say unto thee thou art demon possessed.'' So this man who told me an hour before that I had the glory of God was now telling me that apparently God had a change of heart, and I was in fact demon possessed.

The evangelist started to walk out, but Miranda stood in front of him and blocked the way, demanding an apology. Instead, he lifted up his fist in a threatening manner and said, ''Get out of my way!'' I was devastated and vowed never to go back to that church ever again.

Miranda and I were perplexed and felt like we were never going to find the true church, but God had other plans. We learned a lesson from all of this. Never keep your eyes on man but keep your eyes on Jesus.

Sometime after this, I attended a Christian Businessman's luncheon. Somebody asked me if I would give a testimony. After I did this, I was approached by a member of the Assembly of God Church in Eugene, Oregon. He asked me if I would come to his church and give my testimony there.

Out of this, other doors began opening up. I received honorarium and love offerings for sharing my testimony at different churches and meetings, and the Lord was blessing us. We were finally able to meet our debts and have food on the table.

In the summer of 1970, in a little town south of Grants Pass, I spoke at a community church and a Mrs. Shoemake approached me and asked me if I would be willing to go north, about a hundred miles or so, and speak at her son's church. I agreed to do this.

It was by far the longest journey we had ever taken to speak at a church. Up to this point it had been just a testimony here and there. But this journey had an ultimate destination that we could not see then, for it was the beginning point of what was to become our life's work and ministry — exposing Satan's power!

4

GROWING IN THE LIGHT

Burl Shoemake, the minister of the Church of Christ in Siletz, Oregon, had asked me to come up for several nights. So, Miranda, our little daughter, and I got into the car and drove north. This was really the beginning of what we were later to call E.S.P. Ministries. The name is an acrostic for what we perceived our mission to be— Exposing Satan's Power. It also looks intriguingly similar to the common abbreviation for a well known psychic phenomenon.

Several other ministers had been invited to hear me speak. There was a mixed reaction—some believed me and others did not. The consensus of opinion among those who did not believe me was that Jesus was not doing any miracles today and certainly Satan did not have any power, either. But nowhere in the Bible does it say that Satan's power has finished. Satan is still the god of this world; that is, the world system. As Christians we do not have to worry about these things because "greater is He that is in you than he that is in the world" (I John 4:4).

My message caused controversy. One particular minister at the Church of Christ in Portland, whose name was Gary Strubhar, taped my message and then told me later that he had stayed up most of the night listening to it. Although he found it difficult to believe what I had to say, he could not deny what God's word said. He finally came to the opinion that if God said it, so it must be. Gary Strubhar later played a very important part in helping to get the ministry off the ground.

Burl Shoemake was very helpful and kind. He was primarily responsible for the start of E.S.P. Ministries. Burl suggested that I pack up from where I was living in that converted cowbarn and start life afresh further north. I thought this was a good idea. We had nothing to lose, since I did not have a job anyway.

So we moved up to Siletz. During the journey my car lights failed and we drove the last thirty miles without them. It was quite some drive in the dark and rain along a windy, dangerous road, especially with our U-Haul trailer.

We finally arrived late at night. Burl had hooked up his eight foot wide trailer to the church. That was to be our home for the next several months. Our toilet facilities were in the church so if we wanted to go to the bathroom, we had to get out of the trailer. It often rains in Oregon and we had to go outside even then. That was our lifestyle, but we were happy. I felt that new doors were being opened for me by the Lord.

Burl and I spent a lot of time together and he helped me immensely in learning the Word of God. Other prominent men in my life, such as Ken Edwards, also helped me study the Word. Ken was also instrumental in getting me bookings in Christian churches. Other men who helped were Charles Daily and Norman Fox and there are many more, too numerous to mention here.

Burl had a printing business at the time to help subsidize his ministry and he suggested that I write to churches to tell them about my ministry. He printed 400 letters for me. I sent these letters to churches around the state of Oregon. I received only three replies but I just praised the Lord for these because it was a start.

It is just amazing to me when I think of how the Lord worked in our lives at the times when we were always wondering where the next penny was coming from. God may not always supply our wants but He certainly supplies our needs. He did this unfailingly for us.

For one of my first meetings I had to travel about forty miles to the town of Salem and then on to another little Nazarene church about 100 miles further north. Miranda had told me that we needed $150.00 to live that week. I had only two churches to supply our finances for the whole week.

I will never forget how large the first church seemed to be, and it was packed to capacity. I spoke Sunday morning during the worship hour and then I had a radio speaking engagement that afternoon. I spoke at the church again that evening. The minister then gave me a check from the love offering for $40.00. You can imagine the despair I was in thinking, "Oh, no! How are we ever going to live this week?"

The next day I got in my car and went further north to the little Nazarene church. Just a handful of people showed up at the meeting. The next morning I woke up and the minister gave me breakfast. They gave me some vegetables to help me out and also a check. The check was for $110.00! Praise the Lord! God had given me the money that we needed.

That story could be repeated time after time for the many times things like that happened. But there were some rather funny things, also. I don't know whether you would call them funny "humorous" or funny "peculiar."

One time I had a speaking engagement in Portland, which was a 300 mile round trip. I spoke to 600 people that evening and the church was packed. A love offering was taken and the minister gave me a check for $15.00! But God always took care of us; a perfect example of this being the way He provided us with a home.

Miranda's twin sister Bertha, and her husband had been taking care of her mother in London. Mother was eighty-two years old and not able to care for herself. Bertha's husband had an opportunity for a job which meant moving away from London. Miranda's mother decided she wanted to be with her granddaughter, so she emigrated to America.

Mother sold her home and loaned us enough money to put a down payment on ten acres of land and a mobile home. She then came to live with us in Oregon. This worked out fine and it was exciting for Miranda to have her mother in America.

I will never forget the day Mother arrived. We had to go to Portland International Airport. I had prayed that it would be a nice day, but praying for a nice day in Portland, Oregon, is something else. As usual, it was raining.

Mother looked very distinguished as she came off the plane, waving her hand like the queen does and daintily stepping down the steps into the airport. This was a remarkable eighty-two year old lady immigrating to America. Of course, there was a lot of joy and excitement and Miranda was very happy.

I took photographs and apologized to Mother for the rain. Mother was always very diplomatic and I will never forget her first words. She said, "But my dear chap, didn't it rain in the Bible? Didn't the Bible tell us it rained forty days and forty nights?" I said, "That's right Mother," and I smiled inside for she was trying to be diplomatic, knowing that I was in the ministry, and she wanted to say something about the Bible. Then she said, "By the way, what was the name of that chappy on the boat?" She said this very seriously but we found it hilarious.

Miranda was in her element with ten acres of land and a mobile home. We also had a nice big barn. We were really way out in the boonies, about 150 miles from Portland in a little place called Logsden, Oregon.

Miranda had always wanted animals. One day I came home from a speaking engagement and there in the field stood two animals. I said, "What are those, darling?" She said, "Why dear, they are donkeys and they belong to us. Isn't that marvelous?" I said, "Why two?" and she said, "Well, they need each other for company."

And so it started. First the donkeys and then the next time I came home I said, "What are those things?" These animals were making very menacing noises at me. She said, "These are geese." I asked her what she wanted geese for and she said, "They are marvelous watch dogs."

The next time I saw a sheep and said, "What do you want a sheep for?" "Oh, they keep the grass down so you don't have to mow the lawn." And then there was a goat! I said, "What do you want a goat for?" "Well, that keeps the shrubs and blackberries down so you do not have to worry about them encroaching on you."

And so it went on with ducks, chickens, and what have you. People knew that Miranda liked animals so they were phoning her up and just giving them to her. One day I had a visit from a lady who told me that she had heard me speak and that she wanted to give me a gift. Out trotted this gift on four legs and that was how we got our dog. We also had a horse and then a cat that came to our barn and had its kittens there.

Eventually, Miranda's sister, Bertha, came out with her husband to live with us. We gave them a two acre parcel of land and set them up with a small mobile home. I had double trouble from then on because they collected everything. There was a junkyard near our home and Bertha had a pair of binoculars and would watch the trucks go by. If there was anything good in the truck, she would report to Miranda and they would quickly get into their car and follow the truck.

One day I saw a big truck loaded with boxes come up the driveway, and then my wife and sister-in-law jumped out of it with a gentleman. They said, "Look what we have just been given free—all these boxes!" This huge truck was just stacked with boxes. Then they said, "Guess what? They are filled with rabbits and they are free!"

My wife and her sister were very ecology conscious. The country would spray blackberries to kill them because there were too many. Miranda and Bertha were very upset because insecticides were being used. I remember Bertha coming up the driveway in her car, dust flying everywhere, rushing into the house and calling, "Miranda, the sprayers are coming! The sprayers are coming!" They both ran out of the house, got into the car and drove to the bottom of the field. When the sprayers came, there they stood in front of the bushes with their hands outstretched to stop them. I could not help thinking of the olden days when the famous Paul Revere came in riding his horse and crying, "The British are coming! The British are coming!"

One day, poor old Jenny, our donkey, was wobbling on her last legs. The day of reckoning had come. Miranda did not have the heart to have her put to sleep, so she thought of a bright idea. She suggested that I get a very wide strapping belt, a pulley, and a tackle hoist. We got Jenny into the barn, placed the strapping around her belly, and hoisted her up on her legs. We put the feed under her nose and she ate night and day. In the morning she would be sagging on her knees and it would be my job to hoist her up on her legs.

Life was fun but we still seldom knew where the next penny was coming from. We really lived by faith. In 1970 we had moved from Grants Pass to Siletz. And in August of 1975 we moved to Portland in order to be closer to the airport. It was at this point that we met a delightful couple who became very close to us. Their names were Ron and Toni Sunseri. They had two children—a boy, Chris and their daughter, Nicki. Ron and Toni volunteered their services to us.

Ron was a successful real estate broker. He later gave up a lucrative career to become a preacher. Toni was a highly qualified executive secretary. Their contribution to the ministry was a tremendous asset. Ron also eventually accompanied me to Brazil, South America, and twice to England.

In November of 1977 I moved to Joplin, Missouri, at the suggestion of a dear friend, Knofel Staton. At that time, Knofel was a professor at Ozark Bible College. At the time of this writing he is president of Pacific Christian College, California.

I had been contemplating a move to Joplin for some time, as most of my bookings were coming from the Midwest. This move proved to be very fruitful and our bookings increased. The ministry became very active and this brought me into contact with thousands through speaking engagements and radio and television appearances.

I became a member of the College Heights Christian Church in Joplin. The elders of this congregation graciously offered to oversee the ministry. The following chapter relates some of the most memorable and meaningful experiences that my life's work in the Lord's service has brought to me.

5

THE LIGHT SHINES IN THE DARKNESS . . . . (John 1:5)

Clouds Over Sunny Valley

In the spring of 1970, in Grants Pass, I was approached by a man with an unusual request. He was a Lutheran minister and a local hospital chaplain by the name of Pastor Lang. He related a story about one of his patients, a woman suffering from a traumatic shock resulting from a painful emotional experience.

Her daughter and son-in-law, along with their two children, had disappeared, leaving no forwarding address. This couple was well-educated and had lived comfortably; the son-in-law taught at a university. But they had simply left.

Some months later, the parents were given a copy of *Life* magazine. The front page showed a picture of a family with their backs to the camera. They were looking over their shoulders and smiling. It was with mixed emotions that the parents recognized their daughter, son-in-law, and grandchildren. Why the mixed emotions? The family group was naked.

The magazine carried the feature story describing how this young couple had become fed up with the establishment and had decided to do their own thing. They bought land in Sunny Valley, Oregon and started their own commune.

Anybody and everybody was invited to live there. The motto of the camp was, "If it feels good, then it must be right." Humanism, Spiritism, Atheism and Nudism, along with drugs and sex were all part of the scene. The son-in-law and daughter were the self-styled leaders of this commune.

The parents, who lived in Cleveland, Ohio, immediately set off in their car for Oregon. They located the campsite off the beaten path. They found their daughter and grandchildren. They also saw other men and women. Some residents were clothed and some walked shamelessly around in the nude.

The shock was too much for the mother and she had to be taken to the hospital. Pastor Lang, the chaplain who had brought me her story, promised her that he would do his best to help. He approached me and asked if I would speak to these people in the woods.

I had an idea, so we enlisted the services of the minister of the Community Church in Sunny Valley to accomplish it. The minister had built a good rapport with the commune leader, so we asked him to request permission for me to give a lecture on witchcraft to the commune. A date was fixed and we were invited to a vegetarian dinner with the stipulation that there would be no nudity.

My plan was to speak to them about the intrigues of psychic phenomena, relating to my experiences. Then I would give my testimony of how Jesus changed my life. I planned to tell them what the Scriptures said about witchcraft and its consequences. This was not an experience I could look forward to with great anticipation.

It was with fear and trembling, combined with lots of prayer, that I went to the commune in Sunny Valley. The first person we met seemed to be much older than most of the people there. He stared at me with hatred in his eyes, treating me with contempt and making it clear he disliked me intensely. I then met the leader, who was more cordial; however, his wife was indifferent to me.

Then it was mealtime. It was being cooked outside. There was a young woman with long black hair stirring a large black pot. She looked like a witch stirring her brew. We were then told to form a large circle around this woman and hold hands. There were about seventy people present.

We were then invited to pray. In unison, everybody raised their hands and began to chant. They chanted in ecstatic languages to their Hindu gods. It was hard to believe that in America, a country founded on the Word of God, here in the twentieth century were seventy Americans worshiping idols. It was depressing and degrading and demoralizing. My friend and I looked on with disbelief.

Next, we were given a bowl and spoon and we lined up for our meal. But we ate very little. After dinner we assembled in a log hut. It was filled with beds. Several of the men and women lay on the beds, and some sat on the floor in Yoga positions ready to listen to what I had to say.

I began by relating my experiences. The people were intrigued as they listened and learned about the unholy power and unholy fascination of Satan. Some of these things I am sure they knew about.

Then came the moment of truth. With trepidation and fear, I began to relate from God's Word. I read from the Bible God's abomination of Astrology, Eastern Mysticism, Spiritism and just about every cultic and occultic experience they were involved in. You could have cut the atmosphere with a knife. I spoke to them as kindly as possible, but made it quite clear that unless they quit their activities, they would not enter Heaven.

You can be sure I did not receive a love offering. I walked off the stage wondering what would happen. I could feel one hundred and forty eyes glaring at me. They never expected to hear the gospel along with the occult.

The same man with the icy stare, who met me when I first entered the commune, came up to me. He threatened my life. My friend who was with me was a rather tall, well-built man, something like a linebacker in American football. He raised himself to his full height and was ready to do battle. Praise the Lord for Christian Samsons! When we got out of the commune, we both heaved a sigh of relief. He told me he was scared. I assured him that it was no more than I was.

Looking back, one good thing may have come out of this. A young woman with a child came over just as we were leaving and she thanked me. I pray that the Lord spoke to her heart. However, I never did learn what became of the young family I had gone to see. I pray that the Lord spoke to them also.

"Look, Here Is Water"

In the summer of 1971 I was the missionary speaker at Florence, Oregon. As I lined up for lunch one day with the boys and girls in the camp a young man driving a tractor was cutting the grass alongside us.

Suddenly, he jumped off his tractor and spoke to me. He told me his fiance had listened to me at a meeting I held a year or so ago. He explained to me that he was working his way through medical school and was interested in what I had to say about ectoplasm.

By this time, the lunch line began to move. I invited him to the meeting that evening, but he declined saying he was only at the camp because he was earning money for college. He told me that he was not a Christian and he went on to explain that I could only speak to him at this time because it was his lunch hour. I quickly forgot lunch, collected my Bible, and took him to a quiet spot nearby on the side of the lake.

I began to tell him how I got involved in Spiritualism. He became intrigued. At first he asked questions about ectoplasm, but then came questions about the spirit world and why I had become a Christian. I sensed something was happening to this man. He told me his fiance would often witness to him but he was not convinced that a spirit world existed. Now it was all beginning to make sense to him.

He asked me, "How can I become a Christian?" Throughout this whole conversation I was praying. The Holy Spirit was working in this young man's life. I opened the Bible to the story about Philip and the Eunuch. After I finished reading to him, he pointed to the lake and said, "Look, here is water. Will you please baptize me?"

I was excited and thrilled. I suggested that we go to my cabin and get him a pair of swimming trunks. He said that that was not necessary and since his lunch hour was nearly over, there would not be time. He insisted on being baptized right there and then. So we both went into the lake. He was wearing his work clothes and I baptized him in the name of the Father, the Son, and the Holy Spirit.

I will never forget that precious moment before God. He was a rather tall man and as he came up out of the water he embraced me around the shoulders, looking into the sky and thanking Jesus for eternal life. We walked back to his tractor. The young people were coming out of the dining hall staring at two men, one half wet and the other fully wet. We shook hands and said goodbye. However, that night he returned to the meeting with his fiance and he gave his testimony. Praise the Lord!

Confrontation at Lewis and Clark College

Dr. John Howard, president of Lewis and Clark College, first heard about me through Pastor Lang, the Lutheran minister from Grants Pass. Pastor Lang had read that Dr. Howard was planning a psychic seminar that would include Jeanne Dixon and Hugh Lynn Cayce, son of the world famous Edgar Cayce, now deceased.

Pastor Lang told Dr. Howard about my experiences in Spiritualism but purposely omitted the fact that I was no longer involved in it. He felt that there was more of a chance that the president of Lewis and Clark College would be willing to speak to me.

Dr. Howard wrote me in November of 1971 and invited me to dinner at his home, about 130 miles away. I prayed all the way to Portland that God would give me wisdom to speak to this well-educated man and warn him of the very dangerous position he was in. I was concerned, for this man had the power to introduce thousands of students to witchcraft.

His very gracious wife had prepared an egg souffle and although the meal was delicious, my stomach was in knots. I was thinking about the unpleasant task I had of explaining to this sincere, delightful gentleman how wrong he was in his belief about Spiritualism.

After dinner we retired to the living room. My plan was to tell him how deeply I had been involved in extremes of psychic phenomena. We spoke about clairvoyance, ouija boards, trances, psychometry, materialization and other such things. He was particularly interested in psychic healing because his daughter had an incurable illness.

Dr. Howard was familiar with the rather grotesque phenomenon of ectoplasm and I showed him many slides of it emanating from mediums. He was, to say the least, excited about our discussion.

We talked of some of the rather frightening experiences that I had witnessed in the seance room such as ectoplasm turning to blood, the Bible rising off a table without anyone touching it and then slamming against the wall, the grotesque faces of materialized spirit entities and the resulting fear instilled in our lives.

When asked of his opinion about this, Dr. Howard replied, "No doubt they were evil spirits of the dead." He took the same line that all Spiritualists accept—there are bad spirits we can communicate with, as well as good spirits.

Our discussion continued for several hours, lasting until one o'clock in the morning. Finally, I decided to share my testimony with this gentleman and his wife. They listened while I told of the fear put into my soul by the spirit world of Satan, of the way Satan and Spiritualism had led me into a morbid way of life, and of how it destroyed my marriage and played havoc with my nerves.

I told them of my surprise when I read the Bible and discovered I was headed to eternal damnation. I shared the scripture in Deuteronomy 18:10-12 with them, along with a list of over 100 other scriptures showing God's hatred of all Spiritism. I then pleaded with them to give up this evil and unholy research, to repent, and to trust completely in God.

Mrs. Howard's face had turned white with shock. Dr. Howard's face was ashen, and as he eased himself out of his armchair he said, "In the interest of education, I cannot give up my research of the hereafter." I replied, "Even if it sends you to eternal damnation?" Dr. Howard did not reply. I left, saddened at the thought that Satan had another victim.

KGO San Francisco Radio

In the fall of 1971 my travels took me south to Northern California. On one occasion I had a speaking engagement in the San Francisco area. A local minister got me on the very well-listened-to radio station, KGO - San Francisco.

Initially, the moderator was not sure how the audience would receive my subject so he said that I would have perhaps an hour on the program. As it turned out, I was on the entire three hours that the program lasted. San Francisco is filled with cults and the occult and, of course, homosexuality. The amount of calls that came in was incredible; the switchboard was continuously jammed.

At the beginning of the program I explained what the Bible says about these things, and every call that came in was anti-Christian. It seemed that San Francisco was filled with hate for the Word of God. I had never been under such bombardment in my Christian life.

The moderator, a man by the name of Owen Spann, asked me, "Are you trying to tell me all these people are going to Hell?" I explained to him that I was not the judge and there was always hope for people who were involved in sins of the occult.

He asked me to define sin and I quoted Galatians 5:19, "Now the deeds of the flesh are evident which are immorality, impurity, sensuality, idolatry, sorcery, enmity, strife, jealousy, outbursts of anger, disputes, dissensions, factions, enviousness, drunkenness, carousings, and things like these, which I forewarn you, just as I forewarned you, that those who practice such things should not inherit the Kingdom of God."

I also pointed out I Corinthians 7:9: "Do you not know that the unrighteous shall not inherit the Kingdom of God? Do not be deceived. Neither fornicators, nor idolators, nor adulterers, nor the effeminate, nor homosexuals." At that point he stopped me and said, "Hey, you had better be careful what you are saying. Don't you realize where you are? Are you trying to tell us that homosexuals will not enter heaven?"

I went on to explain that in verse ten of I Corinthians 6, the Bible says, "Nor thieves, nor coveters, nor drunkards, nor revilers, nor swindlers shall inherit the Kingdom of God." I then pointed out verse eleven which says, "Such were some of you, but you were washed, and you were sanctified, but you were justified in the name of the Lord Jesus Christ and in the spirit of God." I was showing that God can forgive the sins of a homosexual or of anyone else when that person becomes a Christian.

Mr. Spann replied that it was impossible for a person who is a homosexual to stop because it has been medically proven to be so. That, of course, is not true. The calls that then came in were all from angry people. Listeners were incensed and the moderator seemed to be enjoying it. Personally, I was not but I was holding my ground. I knew I had the truth.

Finally, an encouraging call came through. The caller was a man who was a former homosexual who had become a Christian. The moderator asked how long the caller had been a homosexual before he became a Christian. He replied that he had been a homosexual for thirty years! The caller then proceeded to give one of the most fantastic testimonies I have ever heard in my life. He shared how he had turned his life over to Christ, and how, with the Holy Spirit working in him, he was able to leave his homosexual life behind. It was exciting to listen to him.

I had planned to drive home that night after my speaking date. As I was getting into the car someone gave me a tape recording of the radio program. I listened to it on the long ride home and I recall being amazed at some of the questions that had been asked. Occasionally, I wondered how a question would be answered and then realized with a jolt that I had already answered it. Truly, it's a miracle how the person of the Holy Spirit brings recall.

That program was the forerunner of many radio and television opportunities. E.S.P. Ministries has recorded about fifty radio and television programs a year in the last fourteen years since that day. We praise the Lord that so many people have been reached by this media.

High on the Holy Spirit

One evening in December of 1971, Jean Houghlam was enjoying a real "high" smoking marijuana. She decided to turn on the radio. As she turned the dial she was intrigued by a British accent. She had turned on a talk show and she began to listen to the conversation between the guest speaker and the listening audience. The guest speaker mentioned that sorcerers would not enter into heaven, and he began to explain what sorcery was.

He explained that the word "sorcery" meant the same as the Greek word pharmakeia, from which we get our word pharmacy. However, what the word in the Bible referred to was actually an enchanted potion.

Several verses in the Bible, such as Deuteronomy 18:10 and Revelation 21:8 and 22:15 describe sorcery in terms of mind-altering drugs, such as marijuana, LSD and heroin. God clearly says that those who take drugs will not enter into heaven.

This was too much for Jean Hougham. She was on the phone like a shot and she told me she smoked maijuana because she got a spiritual high and it drew her closer to God. She was angry. I finally calmed her down and invited her to meet some former hippies, who were once drug addicts but were now Christians. She consented and arrangements were made.

Six months later, I went back to Eugene, Oregon, to speak at the Broadway Church of Christ. An attractive young lady approached me and said, "You are responsible for my becoming a Christian." It was Jean Houghlam.

We corresponded with each other while she served as a missionary in New York and then Italy. Jean Houghlam went from "Unholy Smoke" to the Holy Spirit.

The Phoenix "Fire-Eater"

The plane was circling around the city of Phoenix, Arizona. It was evening and the city looked beautiful from my window seat. The thousands of lights made Phoenix look exciting. Little did I realize how exciting the following evening would be. I was booked for a radio talk show.

My host met me at the air terminal. He was a Mexican gentleman and his name was Emilio Terre-Juarez. He was a successful business man and he greeted me warmly. As we drove from the airport, Emilio turned on the car radio and said, "Ben, I want you to listen to the man who will be your moderator on the talk show tomorrow evening."

Just as the radio came on we heard the host of the show say, "Tomorrow evening's guest will be Ben Alexander, a former Spiritualist medium from London, England. After I have taken care of him, I will toss him to you." The man was rude, crude and offensive.

I thought to myself, "What have I gotten myself into?" My Mexican friend assured me that he was like this to every guest, and he specialized in controversial subjects. He added that this man claimed he never lost a debate and he intentionally tried to make his guests look foolish. However, he had a huge listening audience.

I had met moderators like this before. Their bark was worse than their bite and underneath this veneer they were usually pleasant people. But this man proved to be something else.

The next evening we were ushered into the radio station. Our moderator greeted us with a cigarette dangling from his lips. Much to my distress, he was a chain smoker and the studio was filled with smoke. Emilio sat on my left and my interviewer sat facing me. This was the beginning of a four hour, fire-eating, smoke-filled radio talk show.

My moderator fired the first salvo. "So," he said, "You are a former Spiritualist medium." I replied, "Yes." "And you are trying to tell us that seances were held in the Bible?" he asked. He went on to say, "It so happens that I have a Bible right here." He then handed me a large family Bible that was covered with dust. He said, "So you claim the Bible writes about mediums. Then SHOW ME!" So I opened the Bible to Leviticus 20:27 and showed him: "A man or woman who is a medium or a wizard shall be put to death." This did not please him at all. Then he said, "Seances were held in the Bible? SHOW ME!" So I showed him I Samuel 28, which relates the bringing up of the spirit of Samuel by a medium at the request of Saul.

The moderator began to fire question after question about Spiritualism, fortune tellers, astrologers, and the like, and he kept asking me to prove it by the Bible. I kept doing just that. He kept repeating, "SHOW ME, SHOW ME!" and I kept showing him the Scriptures. He was getting angrier and angrier. He lit cigarette after cigarette. I really thought he was going to have a heart attack.

Suddenly, he took a new line and began denouncing the Bible and Jesus. My Mexican friend was stunned at the moderator's rhetoric and was righteously angry. I had to restrain my friend who told me later that he had wanted to get at this obnoxious man.

Meanwhile, the telephone lines were lighting up. We had already gone one hour into the program. So I suggested that we might take phone calls from the listeners. "Do not tell me how to run my show!" he shouted. All through the program I managed to maintain my composure and this seemed to irritate him. I really felt sorry for him.

He finally decided to take the first call. The caller sounded like an elderly lady. She said to him, "Sir you have insulted my Lord, and I do not appreciate that. I demand an apology." He slammed the receiver down and went to the next caller. The call was for me. After I replied to the gentleman's question, he made the statement that the moderator's behavior was deplorable. I defended the moderator and explained that he was trying to show the viewpoint from the other side. This only served to make the moderator more unhappy and he said, "I do not need you to defend my point of view."

Finally, at midnight, the program closed. The face of the moderator was the color of his burnt cigarettes, ashen grey. Satan really got burned that night.

The Eternal Triangle with the Dead

One of the saddest and most bizarre events in my ministry took place in Lewiston, Idaho, in March of 1973. The minister of the church I was speaking at told me of a woman in the congregation who was seeking a divorce from her husband because she was still in love with her former fiance WHO WAS DEAD!

During my four day presentation, this woman came every night and sat with her head bowed, never looking up during the whole time I spoke. On the last night she remained in her seat after every-- one had left. I sat beside this troubled woman and asked if I could help.

She asked me a question, "Mr. Alexander, if one speaks to the dead can that person still go to Heaven?" I replied, "I am not the judge but the Bible clearly explains that it is detestable to speak to the dead." The Old Testament tells us that it is a sin against God and the penalty in those days was stoning to death, as written in Leviticus 20:27. Also, I pointed out that in I Chronicles 10:13, King Saul died because he consulted with the dead.

She then told me her story. Nineteen years previously she had planned to get married. One week before the wedding her fiance was killed in a car crash. She was grief-stricken and was approached by a group of Spiritualists. She went on to say that during a seance she was hypnotized and had conversed with her now-deceased lover. This affair had continued for nineteen years, despite the fact that she was now married and had two children.

I counseled with her and explained that she was involved in demonism and that I doubted whether she ever did contact her dead fiance. I encouraged her to put her trust in Jesus, and like Isaiah said, "And when they say to you, 'consult the mediums and the wizards who whisper and mutter,' should not people consult their God? Should they consult the dead on behalf of the living?" (Isa. 8:19).

I do not know what finally happened to that poor woman, but I pray she stayed with her family.

Satan Knocked Out in the Last Round

The phone rang and the voice on the other end said, "Mr. Alexander, would you be interested in debating a Spiritualist medium on prime-time television?" The caller identified himself as Lee Tabor, host for a program at 10:30 p.m., Sunday on KOIN television in Portland, Oregon. I agreed and the time and date were set. It was July of 1973.

It was exciting to anticipate hundreds of thousands of viewers not only hearing the exposure of the Devil, but also the Good News of Jesus. My stipulation was that we had to settle on a basis for discussion. I told the moderator I would debate only if the Bible was the final authority. The spirit medium agreed to this. The debate was well-advertised and many Christians were praying that souls would be reached because of this venture.

My strategy for the debate was to treat the whole affair like a prize fight. I would get as many points as I could by quoting the Spiritualist manual and showing where the Bible refutes their doctrines. I planned to eliminate Satan in the last round by a knock-out.

The debate went according to plan. It became apparent early on that the man I was debating knew nothing about the Word of God, and yet he was being interviewed as a "Reverend." (All spirit mediums in America who run a Spiritualist church are called "Reverend.")

The medium, Satan's pawn, was reeling from the might of God's Word. With about five minutes left it was time to deliver the knock-out blow.

I came into the final round with an admission, saying that I realized that seances were held in Old Testament times. King Saul went to a spirit medium at Endor and asked the witch to call up Samuel from the dead.

My opponent took the bait and said, "That proves that the Bible condones Spiritualism." He was exuberant but his joy was short-lived. I retaliated with, "King Saul died because he went to a spirit medium."

"Not in my Bible," the medium said. The moderator then asked him for his Bible, but the medium did not have one with him. I told the moderator, "It's in my Bible," and as I was about to quote I Chronicles 10:13, the moderator snatched the Bible out of my hands and said, "Let me read it." He then read, "So Saul died for his trespass which he committed against the Lord because of the word of the Lord which he did not keep and also because he asked counsel of a medium, making inquiry of it."

The message from the Bible was a devastating indictment against Spiritualism. The moderator turned to the spirit medium and said, "Look, it is true. God says those who go to mediums will die." The medium's Adam's apple bobbed up and down. He was red-faced and speechless. Jesus was victorious!

Letter from the Dead

One evening in the fall of 1973 the phone rang. The voice on the other end said, "Mr. Alexander, I have a problem with a member of the congregation who is involved in the occult. Can you come and hold a meeting for us?" I answered positively and prepared to drive to Bellingham, Washington to hold a three-day meeting.

Early in the meeting, the minister arranged a meeting with two sisters. One was white-faced, extremely nervous, and shaking with fear. The other sister was more composed.

They explained to me how they had lost a brother, who was in his early thirties, in a car accident. Grief-stricken, one sister bought a ouija board and found that the board answered her questions. She believed she was talking to her brother through the ouija board and alleged that he told her to take a pen and his spirit would control her hand to write.

This type of phenomenon is known as automatic writing and can be very convincing evidence of life after death. In this case, the results were amazing. The handwriting was certainly not the sister's but, rather, was identical to the brother's handwriting. The letters supposedly coming from the dead brother, as well as other letters written while he was alive, were taken to a handwriting expert who confirmed that they were written by one and the same person.

The older sister went on to explain that her younger sister had fooled around with the occult ever since she was a teenager and the family feared for her life. She went on to tell me that her sister was told by the spirits that they would no longer use automatic writing. The spirits controlling her were now in a position to communicate by a method known as clairvoyance; this meant she would be able to hear spirits speak. From that point on, the tenor of the message changed. She began to hear nothing but filthy communications during her waking hours and she could not stop this bizarre thing that was happening.

From the time she had started playing with the ouija board her personality had changed. She became withdrawn and had even tried to commit suicide by slashing her wrists. I counseled with her but this was difficult as she would hardly cooperate. The minister promised to take her under his wing and I can only pray that she has since taken refuge in Jesus.

Flight to Freedom

I guess that I have spoken to scores of people on airplane flights that I have taken over the last fourteen years, but none stands out more in my mind than a certain gentleman that I met on a flight from Chicago to Seattle in the spring of 1974.

The plane was packed and I had a center seat. My fellow passenger by the window was a pleasant-looking young man. We began talking and he asked me about my vocation. "What a golden opportunity," I thought, and I whipped out my calling card, which was a thirty-two page comic strip depicting my life story.

The young man, Bruce McIntosh, was impressed and intrigued as he read the little booklet. Then he noticed in the story that I was Jewish and he became more interested. He told me that he was Jewish, too, but did not believe in God.

"Why do you believe there is a God?" he asked. I thought, "Praise the Lord! I have three hours to tell him and he is a captive audience."

I began with my involvement in Spiritualism and the intriguing, but frightening, reality of the spirit world. I then went on to explain how my life was changed after I became a Christian. I encouraged him to consider Christianity.

About a year later, I received a letter from this young Jewish man. He wrote, "You probably do not remember me, but I was the atheist

Jew you met on the plane from Chicago to Seattle." I certainly did remember him! He went on, "I want you to know that on that flight you sowed a seed and now I am a Christian."

Praise the Lord! I am not sure of the airline, but it was surely a flight bound for Heaven.

From Witchery to Missionary

Gene Sonnenberg was involved in a campus ministry in St. Joseph, Missouri. He invited me to speak there in September of 1975. While there, he introduced me to Sherry Elliot, a young woman who attended meetings at the Campus House.

Sherry claimed to have been a witch since the age of thirteen years. She said she had become a Christian but now her life was in turmoil. Sherry was being told by a group of Pentecostals that although she was a Christian, she needed to confess her sins and have the demons cast out of her.

She explained that her Pentecostal friends were exorcising demons from her body. The poor girl was spiritually and emotionally confused. She questioned her salvation and was very depressed over the whole confusing situation.

Gene and I counseled with her and showed her from God's Word what she needed to do to be assured that she belonged to Jesus.

1. The First Step: Hearing (Rom. 10:17)
2. The Second Step: Faith in Jesus Christ (Heb. 11:6)
3. The Third Step: Repentance of Sin (Acts 17:30)
4. The Fourth Step: Confession (Matt. 10:32)
5. The Fifth Step: Burial with Christ by Baptism
                      - immersion in water (Rom. 6:3, 4 and
                      Acts 2:38)
6. The Sixth Step: Live a godly life (II Peter 1:5-8)

Sherry obeyed the Lord on all points. I had the honor of baptizing her that night.

About a year or so later, I received a letter from Taiwan, China. I was thrilled, for it was from Sherry. She now serves as a missionary in that country and keeps me informed of her activities on a regular basis. Praise the Lord!

Brazil

The stamp on the envelope showed that the letter came from Brazil. It was an invitation to speak to a group of missionaries in January of 1977.

What a wonderful opportunity to speak in a country that boasted of the largest number of Spiritualists in the world—twenty million, in fact. I jumped at the chance and readily accepted. I invited my friend, Ron Sunseri, to come with me. We had to raise our fare and wondered how we would even manage to do so, but manage we did. Ron and I flew to Belem, Brazil.

It was not a very auspicious beginning. An official boarded the airplane and sprayed all the passengers with some kind of bug killer.

We had no problem with customs, simply because Varig Airlines had left our bags in Miami. We did not receive them till four days later. With 100% humidity and no change of clothes in the hot, sticky weather, you can imagine that even best friends kept their distance. Even so, it was great fun to be fellowshiping and lecturing to our wonderful missionaries.

One of the other guest speakers was a former spirit medium from that country. It was interesting to note that he spoke Portuguese and no English while I spoke English and no Portuguese. Yet after our lectures, the missionaries compared notes and discovered that our experiences were similar in many instances. Spiritualism is universal and the phenomena have basic principles.

After a week of speaking, my plans called for going to Brazilia, the new capital city of Brazil. I had planned to fly but some of the missionaries asked me to accompany them on the bus. This way, they said, I could stop on the way and preach to their congregations.

They also assured me it would be a pleasant, comfortable ride. The seats in the bus were, in fact, comfortable, but what they neglected to tell me was how the sanitary convenience worked. For some reason, when the toilet was used the whole bus suffered.

I will never forget the restaurants on that trip, either. The first one we stopped at had no doors or windows. Dogs wandered in and out among the tables looking for scraps. They surely got plenty to eat at our table.

A waiter came around with a large roast on a skewer. We have a television commercial in this country where three elderly ladies are looking at a huge hamburger roll with a very tiny patty on it and one of the ladies remarks, "Where's the beef?" When we looked at the skewer in the waiter's hands we might have said the same thing for the meat was covered with millions of flies.

The waiter took a sharp knife and sliced pieces of meat, along with the flies, onto our plates. Needless to say, the dogs never went hungry, but Ron and I did. The missionaries never blinked an eye; they just ate. It made me keenly aware of the fact that it takes a special kind of person to be a missionary.

Finally, we arrived in Brazilia. We found this city to be a marked contrast to Belem and many other places in Brazil. The buildings and houses were quite modern and they were occupied mainly by government workers.

The minister in Brazilia, David Saunders, invited me to speak to his congregation. I discovered that Brazilians, who are delightful people, have no sense of time. They were coming in at all times during the service.

During the service, one lady seemed ill at ease. She would get out of her seat, walk to the back of the church, then come back again and sit down. Ron Sunseri later told me he was watching this lady and he noticed that each time I mentioned what God's Word said about Spiritualism, she would become agitated. He also noted from the symbols on her brooch and necklace that she was a Spiritualist. Ron was praying for her.

Finally, at the end of the message I extended an invitation and, praise the Lord, she accepted and came down the aisle. Through an interpreter, I explained God's plan of salvation and she enthusiastically accepted Jesus as her Savior.

I had the privilege and honor of baptizing Maria Kourt into Christ.

Freda Gets Off the "Tract"

In the early days of the ministry I always traveled by car. We had a Plymouth Fury that we had nicknamed Freda. Freda had one big problem which was that her roof leaked. We always got wet when it rained but Freda's dependability never failed us. Freda and I traveled many miles together and then her age began to tell on her. She suffered in just about all of her mechanical joints.

On one trip from Logsden, Oregon, to Arcata, Freda and I both got drenched in the rain—Freda on her outside and me on her inside. Poor Freda not only got wet but she suffered a seizure as well and became completely immobilized.

After being towed by a wrecker, Freda was diagnosed as having something akin to what we would experience as appendicitis. She was in need of a transmission transplant, a very expensive operation, and would be hospitalized for two or three days. In my circumstances there was no way that I could have a second opinion.

Since I was on my way to a speaking engagement that evening, I phoned the minister at the church where I was expected and explained my dilemma. He agreed to drive down the hundred mile trip and get me.

There was a cafe nearby and I went in to have a cup of coffee while I waited. Rather than waste time as I sat there, God prompted me to doodle on a napkin. That doodling worked itself into my first tract called "The Ouija Board."

Freda's breakdown turned into a blessing and the results of the writing of that tract were to become known to me in a most dramatic way.

The Ouija Board That Asked Too Much

While I was speaking in a church northwest of Portland, Oregon, I spotted a Christian magazine. The cover featured an article called "The Ouija Board That Asked Too Much," written by Marian Duckworth. The name of the magazine was *Christian Life* and it was the March, 1977 issue. Here are some excerpts from the article.

> Donna Duncan took the Ouija board from its box on the shelf and placed it on the dining room table of their Spokane, Washington home where her husband Allen and their two daughters, Beth, 12 and Mellany, 9 sat waiting. There was no sound; radio or TV would have disturbed their concentration.
>
> Donna began. She rested her fingers lightly on the pointer and asked the question that opened each session. "Do you come in the white light

of the Lord?'' The answer came immediately, ''Yes!'' The pointer slid along the board, moving from letter to letter spelling out words and sentences in the strange, supernatural way that had mesmerized the Duncans for months and had kept them at the board slavishly night after night.

At 9:00 p.m. Beth and Mellany left for bed. Donna and Allen stayed on as they nearly always did, working the board alone while the gold sunburst clock on the wall ticked the hours away. At midnight the Duncans were still at the table asking the board questions and watching, enthralled, as it spelled out answers. Occasionally, Donna stopped to enter one of the board's messages in her diary. Finally, at nearly 1:00 a.m. they went to bed. ''The board became the greatest force in our lives!'' Donna said. ''We lived by it. We believed that through it Jesus Christ, Himself was speaking to us.''

A year before, Donna had been invited to join friends who gathered regularly to work a Ouija board. The rec room seemed chilly that evening, and she shivered as she sat drinking hot coffee and watching the board spell out messages. She knew that these people claimed to have contacted spirits who sometimes spoke through table tapping as well as through the Ouija board.

''Come on, Donna,'' they urged. ''Sit in this time. Try it yourself.'' Were they making the pointer move or were their fingers really moving supernaturally? Frightened but fascinated, she sat down with the others . . . and discovered that the pointer spelled out messages without being pushed by those present.

Soon the Duncans moved to another part of Spokane and away from the friends who had introduced Donna to the Ouija board. But about a year later, while she was serving on a school committee, she met another Ouija board enthusiast.

''The woman told me that she got together with several friends and family members and worked the board and that they had contacted relatives who had died,'' Donna said. ''The longer she talked, the more she aroused my curiosity . . . I wanted one for myself.'' When Allen came home, Donna asked if he thought she should buy one. ''I do not think it would matter what I told you; you would buy one anyway,'' he told her.

That night, the Duncans' five month obsession with the Ouija board began. She had been praying that her family would become Christians and continued to pray for them all during their Ouija board experiences. What did the Duncans believe about Satan and demons? An evil spirit called Satan existed they knew. He was abstract, though, and totally unrelated to their lives in the Northwest. "Demon" was just a word to them, like "witch" or "spirit."

But through what the Duncans supposed was just a game like Monopoly or checkers, Satan moved into their lives. No secret ceremonies with strange incantations; just a mass-produced game board and a Bible on the bookshelf of Twentieth-century America.

Ouija became a kind of religious exercise, for the Duncans believed that this was God's way for them to communicate with the spirit world and with Him. The day really began when their fingers were moved across the board by an unseen force and they asked the question they had been told was for their protection: "Do you come in the white light of the Lord?"

Although at first the Duncans invited others to work the board with them, it did not respond as well with others present, so their evenings became private times. The board continually urged them to hold a seance, but Allen was reluctant and was afraid of the occult and refused.

Then one evening the board spelled out these words, "I have a pleasant surprise. Someone wants to speak with you." "Do you come in the white light of the Lord?" "Yes! I am Jesus, the Son of God!" Donna says, "We really thought we had been specially chosen." Often after that when the Duncans asked, "Who is on the board?" the answer came back, "I am the Lord!"

About five months after Donna first bought the Ouija board home, Bertha Taylor, a Christian neighbor, stopped in and found the Duncans bent over the board. "Bertha looked terrified," Donna recalls. "What you are doing is really dangerous. It is against what the Word of God says," she told us. Bertha left but soon came back with a tract written by Ben Alexander, once a trance medium himself. He had come to the United States from England to begin a Spiritualist organization. Instead, he became a Christian and had written this severe warning against the use of the Ouija board.

"I sat down and read it immediately," Donna said. "The fact that I read it at all was a miracle because I was so wrapped up with what the board was doing that I was just sure it was being used by God." The tract quoted Ephesians 6:12: "For we are not fighting against people made of flesh and blood, but against persons without bodies—the evil kings of the unseen princes of darkness who rule this world; and against huge numbers of wicked spirits." It also warned against trying to contact people who were dead. It quoted Deuteronomy 18:10, 11: "There must not be found among you anyone who makes his son or daughter pass through fire, a diviner, a soothsayer, an augur, a sorcerer, a charmer, a medium, a magician, or a necromancer." (A necromancer is one who contacts the dead.) It went on to say, "We see, therefore, that Ouija boards, sorcery, and all forms of Spiritualism can be nothing but a way of having communication with demons, and are against Scripture. It is forbidden by God and considered by Him to be defiling. So why go to the Ouija board when you can go directly to Jesus Christ?"

For the first time since she had become obsessed with the board, Donna was sick with fear. Had she been communicating with the demons of Satan and supposing them to be of God? Had Satan been impersonating Jesus Christ?

When Allen came home that night, she showed him the tract. "As soon as I have finished dinner, I will read it and then question the board about it," he said. So after supper the Duncans sat down at the board as usual. "What do you want from us?" Allen asked it. Without any hesitation the board spelled out, "Your souls." "I'm sorry but you are not going to get them," Allen replied. The pointer went from Ha! to Ha! "No," Allen said, "the last laugh is going to be on you." With that, Allen rose from the table and together he and Donna threw the Ouija board into the fireplace and watched the flames consume it.

I eventually contacted Allen and Donna Duncan. They had moved to a town just outside Seattle, Washington. I introduced them to Dale Siepp, a minister in the area, and they became members of the church.

Satan Gets Burned

I had said goodnight to all the folks at the meeting in Valparaiso, Indiana one August night in 1977, and I noticed one gentleman who waited till everyone left. He came over and said, "Mr. Alexander, my name is Don Young. I am a Mormon and a Spiritualist." He went on to explain that he had been a spirit medium for about thirty years and was shocked at what the Bible had to say about Spiritualism. He really believed his gift of mediumship was from God.

Don Young was a frightened man and he bombarded me with questions. All of these I answered with God's Word. He then asked me, "What shall I do?" So I opened God's Word and showed him the plan of salvation. I emphasized the eight conversions in the book of Acts.

He then told me that he had many books and fetishes. (A fetish is a material object believed to be the dwelling place of a spirit.) He wanted to know what to do with them. I point out to him in Acts 19:19 that many of those who practiced sorcery brought their books together and began burning them in the sight of all. They counted up the price of them and found it to be fifty thousand pieces of silver. This verse of Scripture left an impression on him and he promised to think things over. He also said he would return the following evening.

Prayers were offered for Don Young. The following evening I awaited with anticipation the return of this bewildered soul. I was excited and I looked for Don. The church began to fill up but there was no sign of him. I spoke that evening with a heavy heart.

When I finished, I requested the minister to give an invitation to the congregation. Suddenly, a man walked past me, going down the aisle. I looked twice—it was Don Young, praise the Lord! He had given his heart to Jesus.

Don asked me if I would baptize him. I assured him I would consider it a blessing. While we were undressing, he became afraid. His fears concerned his Mormon background. I had discussed this problem with him the previous night, showing him the errors of the Mormon religion. Finally, he was baptized. The whole church had waited for this moment and applause broke out all over the building. How I love to see people react like this to a new soul won for Christ!

Don and I dressed, and suddenly he turned and said, "Do you know what happened this evening? I arrived in time for church but a voice kept telling me not to go in, that I would be sorry." Then he told me how he kept driving around and around in his car. Finally, he prayed, parked the car, and walked into the church. He had then come forward to be baptized.

After the baptism he asked me rather strangely if I would accompany him to his car. He wanted to show me something. I was not too sure about this and I asked him if he would also show two of the Elders who were standing with us. I really felt that where two or three are gathered together—IT'S SAFER! (By the way, that is not a Scripture verse.)

We all trooped outside and he led the way to his car. He opened up the trunk and brought out an attache case and a can of gasoline.

He opened the case and it was filled with witchcraft books of every description. There were also all kinds of weird fetishes. He laid them out on the parking lot, poured the gasoline all over them and set fire to them.

Praise the Lord! We were witnessing Acts 19:19 taking place again in the Twentieth Century.

The Chosen One

The meeting was over rather late that evening, but there was still a long night ahead of me. It was May, 1979, and I had a radio talk show appearance scheduled in Fort Wayne, Indiana, starting at midnight. My host kindly consented to take me on the long journey to the studios of WOWO radio.

We arrived just in time and were ushered to the top floor of the building. The moderator boasted of his large audience and explained that his was a fifty thousand watts station.

The talk show began. I explained to the listeners what Spiritualism was and told them of its many subtle by-products. I warned them of the dangers of the occult. The phone lines were opened up and immediately there was a flood of calls. At about 2:00 a.m., a caller protested that he had been phoning for two hours to get through. I was not surprised for the lines were lit up all through the program, which lasted till 3:00 a.m.

The man gave his name as Tim and said that he was heavily involved in everything I had warned the listeners about. He was especially shaken by what the Bible said about the occult. Because he was allowed such a short time on the radio, he requested my address, which I was only too happy to give. True to his word, I received a letter from him within a few days. It was heartbreaking to read how he had destroyed his life.

He had had an executive position with the Morton Salt Company. He had had a lovely wife and four daughters. He had owned several cars, a very nice home, and had some other investments in property. Life had, indeed, been good to him.

Because of his work, he entertained frequently. One day he bought a ouija board to amuse his guests. To his surprise, he found the silly thing worked. He was fascinated and captivated with the information the ouija board gave him. Eventually, the messages on the ouija board told him to take a pen and the spirits would communicate by writing through him. This phenomenon is a form of automatic writing. The spirits explained that this form of communication would be much quicker.

The spirits controlling him then told him that he was a chosen vessel of God, that he had been chosen to write a book. After a time of automatic writing, his spirit guide told him to go to the typewriter. Tim said that his fingers literally flew across the keys. Tim became totally obsessed with his new-found powers. He neglected his work and he was fired. He neglected his wife and children and became divorced. He lost everything.

After receiving his letter, I wasted no time and contacted him by phone. His biggest surprise was that anybody cared. Fortunately, I had an upcoming meeting in his vicinity and I promised I would visit him very shortly. I contacted a friend of mine by the name of Jerry Paul, who is the minister of the Georgetown Church of Christ in Fort Wayne, Indiana. Jerry agreed to accompany me to see this man.

Tim lived just a few miles from the church. Arrangements were made by phone to meet him. We drove to a rundown neighborhood and arrived at his home. Jerry and I prayed before we went in. Tim certainly looked to be in a sorry state. What had happened to this man who had once owned properties, cars, and a lovely home and who had once had a loving family? Satan, as only he can do, had torn this man's life apart. He was living in the same house with a divorcee and her daughter. I felt sorry for this unkempt, unshaven man.

However, he was glad to see us. He just found it difficult to believe that people cared and he often mentioned this to us in our conversation. Tim quickly got into his story. He showed us reams of typewritten papers belonging to the book he was writing under the spell of his spirit guide. He went on to discuss other matters which I am not at liberty to tell of. As far as he was concerned, his spiritual and physical needs were completely met through his spirit guides. It was bizarre, to say the least. Jerry Paul sat throughout listening to this man, spellbound. It seemed inconceivable that right here in the heart of the Bible Belt, witchcraft was being practiced in an American home.

I then went into detail explaining what God's Word says on the occult. Tim was visibly disturbed. He agreed to stop all communication with the spirit world.

Then Jerry Paul witnessed to Tim in the most beautiful way that I have ever seen or heard. Jerry promised he would help if Tim really wanted to be helped. Also, Jerry stressed that Tim would have to cooperate. Tim indicated that he knew he was in a mess and that he would do anything to get out of his predicament.

Later on, I learned that Jerry spent many long hours with Tim and his lady friend, counseling, studying, and praying with them. Nine months later I was speaking in a church in Topeka, Kansas. Suddenly, the siren for warning to take shelter sounded. A tornado had touched down and was heading in our direction. The sky turned a strange dirty-yellow and looked stormy. Hailstones as big as golfballs hit the roof, and we ran down into the basement.

While this was taking place, a phone call from Fort Wayne, Indiana came through to me. It was Jerry Paul and he said, "There is someone here who wishes to speak to you." The voice on the other end said, "This is Tim Ducey. I want you to be the first to know that I am just about to be baptized." He went on to say that Jerry had worked tirelessly with him for the past nine months and Jerry had also performed a wedding ceremony for Tim and his girlfriend. She had been baptized just a few weeks before, and now Tim was making his decision for Jesus Christ as well.

Praise God for men like Jerry Paul. Thanks to his Christian love and dedication, Tim had truly become a "chosen one."

Sears and Roebuck

In September of 1980, Miranda was looking at a brochure advertising magazines which was sent in the mail to us by Sears and Roebuck. "Ben," she said, "look what Sears and Roebuck are selling." The inducement to buy was a chance to win a $100.00 prize. What upset my wife was the fact that one of the magazines being offered was the porno rag *Playboy.*

I became angry and immediately reached for the phone. I called long distance to the Sears Tower in Chicago. "This is Ben Alexander calling long distance for the President," I said. "What do you wish to speak to him about?" came the response. I replied, "I am sorry but this is a personal message for the President only." I have learned that when a man receives a phone call and is told that it is personal, he usually cannot resist satisfying his curiosity about who it might be and what they might want.

I was then put through to the man in charge of the magazine promotion, a Mr. Pugh. He said, "Sears has a magazine promotion twice yearly and we have never had a complaint before." He also believed that *Playboy* was a work of art. I was flabbergasted. He indicated to me that *Playboy* was his best seller and he had no intention of taking it off the market. In fact, he was quite upset that I would even suggest it.

I said, "Mr. Pugh, if you do not take it off the market I will no longer patronize Sears. What's more, I send out 12,000 newsletters to families all over the United States, and 6,000 of these newsletters go to churches with memberships anywhere from fifty to 2,000 people." I told him that I planned to inform my readers that Sears was selling *Playboy.* I also had plans to start a nation-wide advertising campaign. I placed more phone calls to Sears telling them I meant business. I hate pornography with a passion.

Finally, I received a letter from the Vice-President of the company and I am thankful to Sears for the stand they took against pornography. The letter reads as follows:

SEARS, ROEBUCK AND CO.
Sears Tower
Chicago, Illinois 60684

National	C.W. Harper
Headquarters	Vice-President
	Public Relations Dept.

September 30, 1980

Mr. Ben Alexander
P.O. Box 1723
Joplin, MO 64801

Dear Mr. Alexander:

I regret Sears has offended you by a recent magazine subscription promotion, which included *Playboy* as one of the offerings.

I want you to know that Sears is proud of its reputation as a store for the entire family. We intend to continue and strengthen that reputation. In keeping with this tradition, we will not offer *Playboy* magazine subscriptions again.

We appreciate your letter voicing concern. Please be assured we hope to continue serving you in a manner that meets the highest standards.

Sincerely yours,

C.W. Harper

I saw in this letter, as in many of the incidents I have related in this chapter, a visible sign that God was blessing the efforts of my ministry. But somewhere in the back of my mind I felt an uneasy nagging. Even after all the years of doing the Lord's work, my past life still haunted me. I could sense that a time of confrontation between past and present, between darkness and light, needed to take place.

6

...BUT THE DARKNESS HAS NOT UNDERSTOOD IT (John 1:5)

For some time I had been planning to return to England. I had several reasons for wanting to do this. First, there was Stewart; I wanted to be reunited with my son. I had already made several trans-Atlantic telephone calls to him. I am happy to say that Stewart now lives in Florida with his wife, and that we have a closer relationship.

Secondly, I was anxious to witness to my old acquaintances in London at the Spiritualist Association. Finally, I was curious to know what had happened to Jeff Miller, and I wanted very much to get from him the photographs of psychic phenomena that we had taken in the seance room.

So in November of 1974, I took my first trans-Atlantic flight to England, having traveled by sea the other times. I flew from Portland to Chicago, where I boarded a Trans World Airlines flight to London. Many thoughts crossed my mind during that journey. I wondered how my son would accept me and how he would look. I had not seen him for ten years; he was now twenty-six. I was also thinking about meeting with Jeff Miller. That thought brought back fears; especially when I remembered the threatening letters I had received from that Satanic circle.

The plane touched down at Heathrow Airport in London and I took a bus to my hotel in Ilford, a suburb just outside the city. There I met Stewart and we spent several happy days together. I then had the rather dubious task of confronting some old friends from my days in Spiritualism.

Armed with tracts and prayers, I made my way to 33 Belgrave Square, the address of the headquarters of the largest Spiritualist organization in the world. I met several old acquaintances and after exchanging a few pleasantries, I got down to the task of showing them God's Word about Spiritualism. I can sum up the outcome of that crusade by telling you how the president of the Spiritualist Association of Great Britain, Mr. Hunter Macintosh, replied to me.

After he rejected God's Word on Spiritualism, I quoted to Mr. Macintosh, "There is a way that seems right," and before I could finish my sentence he said to me, "Don't quote me the Bible. I know 'there is a way that seems right to a man but its end is the way of death'" (Prov. 14:12). He then went on to tell me that the Bible had been distorted to favor the case against Spiritualism and, futhermore, Spiritualists get the truth about life after death at seances from ministers who have died.

The apostle Paul said, "The one whose coming is in accord with the activity of Satan, with all power and signs and false wonders, and with all the deception of wickedness for those who perish because they did not receive the love of the truth so as to be saved. And for this reason God will send upon them a deluding influence so that they might believe what is false" (II Thess. 2:9-11). How true this statement is. I regret that Hunter Macintosh is a typical example of the Spiritualist belief. I left, a saddened man.

My time in London was running out and I had not located Jeff Miller. I found a local church near the hotel where I was staying and I decided to go. The people were friendly and inquired about where I was from. I gave them the tract published by Life Messengers about my life story. One family became interested and invited me home for lunch. I explained my mission and told them how anxious I was to locate Jeff Miller. I spent most of the day telling them about my experiences in Spiritualism, especially the intriguing involvement with Jeff. My new-found Christian friend said he would help me to find

Jeff the next day. I was getting desperate, as I had to return to the United States on Tuesday, so I was grateful for the offer.

The next day after work, my friend picked me up in his car and we drove to Darnel Road, Stoke Newington. I located the house and knocked on the door. A stranger answered and told us that the Miller's had moved and left no forwarding address. The people next door did not know their whereabouts, either.

There was only one more link left and that was Joe Coleman, the elderly gentleman who had attended the seances hoping to hear from his dead wife. This meant a trip to Hackney, a borough about five miles away. Then began a two hour search. London had changed; new flats had been built and it was difficult for me to remember landmarks around where Joe had lived. I was about to give up when I spotted a small passage-way leading to a church. That was it! Joe Coleman's house was at the rear of the church. I was elated as we walked down the passage and found Joe's house.

Joe did not recognize me at first. But he then invited us in and we visited a while. Joe related to my friend the ventures into Spiritualism that I had already told him about. He then told us where Jeff lived. And he went on to say that Jeff's mother had been killed in a motor vehicle accident in 1974. But the most interesting news was that Jeff was now being used by the spirits for psychic surgery. This phenomenon I had never seen, nor did I wish to. But I had seen enough ectoplasmic materializations to quite easily accept the reality of this.

I asked Joe Coleman if he had any photos. He told me Jeff had all the pictures and, in any case, I would have to get permission to take them through Mr. Richards, the demon spirit who still controlled Jeff Miller. My new friend was quickly learning about the control Satan has over people's lives.

But time was now at a premium and I needed to see Jeff. It was about 11:30. Jeff had not moved too far from his other home so we made it to his place by midnight. We rang the bell and after what seemed to be an eternity, I could hear somebody coming down the stairs shouting at us very angrily. This was my introduction to Carol, Jeff's wife.

I explained who I was and that I was leaving for the States the next day. She was pretty mad but she allowed us to follow her up the dingy, winding staircase to the top floor. Suddenly, she turned and said, "I remember now, you are the one that ran out of the seance." My friend looked at me and whispered, acknowledging what I had told him about the frightening experience I had at my last seance.

We went into the tiny apartment and Jeff was delighted to see me. I told him that I was a Christian minister, but never let on that I was against Spiritualism. I must admit that I felt ashamed that I didn't tell him this. I felt I needed more time, and I was also anxious to get the photos of the materializations. These were important to me as further evidence to Christians back home of the reality of these things.

I asked Jeff if he would let me have the photographs to take back to show my friends in America. Jeff said, "Sorry, Ben, I will have to get permission from Mr. Richards." I was not about to wait until Jeff went into a trance to talk to one of Satan's disciples, so I gave Jeff my address in America and he promised to send the photos if Mr. Richards approved.

I was disappointed and reluctantly said goodbye. Meanwhile, my conscience was bothering me. Here was a soul in the clutches of Satan and I hadn't offered Jeff Miller the way out. I had allowed Satan to trick me into being afraid.

Soon after I arrived back in America, I wrote to Jeff and sent him all my literature about what the Bible says on the occult. I also invited him to come and stay with me in America. Jeff did not answer. I did not discover the outcome of my sending that letter until five years later, when I once more returned to England.

The thought of Jeff and his situation plagued me constantly. Since he had not answered my letter, I was concerned about how he had taken it. I must admit I was nervous, too. I was positive that the spirit entities who controlled Jeff would do everything in their power to destroy me.

Finally, five years later, unable to ignore my conscience any longer, I began to make plans to return to England. I would see Jeff Miller face to face and tell him how he was being used by Satan. Ron Sunseri agreed to accompany me. He considered it a fact-finding trip and intended to keep a diary. In December, 1979, we flew to London.

Our plans called for me to speak at several churches in London and Birmingham. Fred Miller, a missionary in England, met us at the airport and drove us to his home and church in Streatham. His wife, Charlotte, was very gracious and took good care of us. We made Streatham our headquarters and I spoke at several churches while in London.

The most important assignment was to see Jeff Miller again and so it was with mixed feelings that Ron and I made our way to the East Side of London. We decided first to visit my old friend, Joe Coleman, and feel him out as to what reaction Jeff had had to the letter I sent him five years ago. It was not difficult this time to find Joe's place.

Joe was happy to see me and I introduced Ron to him. Ron asked if he could tape what was being said, as Ron was interested in psychic phenomena. Joe was only too pleased to cooperate. Joe told us that when Mrs. Miller had died, the phenomena of materializations stopped altogether and Jeff was being used by the spirits for psychic surgery. Joe then produced a small jar with something that looked like a piece of flesh in alcohol. I must confess I had never seen Jeff perform psychic surgery, but as I have stated before, after witnessing many Satanic miracles, I found no difficulty in accepting this as fact.

Joe told us that Jeff's wife, Carol, no longer attended the seances, as the sight of blood made her ill. He said that Jeff, himself could not stand the sight of blood, either. Jeff never saw how the operations took place because he was always in a trance. When it was all over and he had come out of the trance there would be blood on his hands. Jeff had taken to drinking and the spirit guides could use him more easily because he had little or no control over himself.

We left Joe Coleman's house and made our way to Stoke-Newington where Jeff lived. We rang the bell several times but nobody answered. Finally, a couple who were going out came down and told us we would find the Millers on the top floor. Ron and I climbed the stairs and knocked on the door. Jeff answered and, much to my relief, he threw his arms around me like an old and welcomed friend.

After I introduced Ron to Jeff, Jeff began to pour out his heart to me. He apologized for being a little drunk and told us that life meant very little to him now. He said that if he had only five minutes more to live, the spirits would use him. He complained he was being tormented constantly, and that his life was completely controlled by spirit entities. He would put a cassette in a tape recorder, press the record button, and then go into a trance. The spirit would speak through him into the tape recorder and give him instructions on how to live. Ron and I felt sorry for this poor soul.

I told Jeff that the reason I came to see him again was because the last time we met I did not have the courage to tell him that Spiritualism was of the Devil. Now I had come back to tell him face to face. Jeff told me that when he got my letter the spirits who controlled him were seething with anger and told him to pretend that he would become a Christian and to accept my invitation to come to America. Then at an opportune moment, when Jeff and I were alone, the spirits would take Jeff over with a savage entity and, while he was in a trance, they would take my life.

Under the influence of an evil spirit, a letter was written accepting my invitation. Jeff took the letter to the post office and stood in line to have it weighed. While in the line, he suddenly felt nervous and tried to light a cigarette. He lit match after match but could not light the cigarette. He had been sixth in line when he came in and by the time he was second, he was so embarrassed that he walked out and never did mail the letter. I believe God in his providence made sure that Satan would not have his way that day.

Jeff then told us he had to leave soon because he had to hold a seance across town. He said he was forced to go because that was his only means of earning money to keep body and soul together. Ron and I both volunteered to give him money to stop him from going to the seance. Jeff agreed to stay at home and we spent the whole day praying and teaching him about Jesus.

Towards evening Carol came home. Jeff warned us that she would not speak to us until she had a cup of tea. He explained that she hated her work and needed to be alone until she recovered from the trauma of it. When Ron and I first saw her, we both thought, "What a poor, wretched woman, and what a way to live!"

Carol truly was a most miserable woman. She hardly spoke to us and when she did, she spent most of the time complaining. I suggested that instead of her cooking a meal, we would like to take them out to supper. This idea brightened her up and we took them to a Jewish restaurant. We then had an opportunity to discuss plans for them to visit America and get involved in the Christian way of life. They both liked the idea but were suspicious. I believe they were suspicious because we had asked them for photographs of ectoplasm emanating from Jeff's body. Jeff said he would give them to us when they arrived in the United States. We assured them we had no ulterior motives other than to see them both come to Christ. That evening we left praising the Lord and anticipating the snatching of a very powerful soul and his wife away from Satan.

Ron and I spent a long time on our knees that evening. The following night we visited with Jeff and Carol and explained to them the battle that they were involved in. In Ephesians 6:12 the apostle Paul explains that our fight is not against human beings, but against "principalities, powers, and rulers of darkness." On the other side there is the Spirit of God, the Holy Spirit, and man's mind is the battleground of these two forces. I explained that in order to be delivered from this course of Satan, they would have to obey the gospel.

They admitted that they needed to repent, but they steadfastly refused to be baptized. While we were witnessing to them, I realized from the expression on Jeff's face that he was going into a trance. Suddenly, a picture that was hanging on the wall unhooked itself and flew several feet across the room and landed on the floor by Jeff's side.

Jeff calmly picked it up and in a trance-like voice said, "Mr. Richards wants to speak to us." Immediately, Carol jumped up and went over to Jeff and shook him out of his trance. Ron was witnessing for the first time something that I had experienced for years. His face was as white as a sheet and fear showed in his eyes. Later, he said to me, "Ben, I always believed you but when I saw that picture sailing across the room, it confirmed everything you had ever said."

Satan was doing all he could to hang on to Jeff's soul. Ron and I prayed. We were meeting the enemy face to face. We were invading his territory, but we were determined to win this couple to Christ. We finished our lesson and Satan, himself, provided the illustration for us. We won the battle that night because of Jesus. "Greater is He that is in you than he that is in the world" (I John 4:4).

We introduced Jeff and Carol to Fred and Charlotte Miller, the missionaries who had housed us, in hopes that they would go to their church. However, they made the excuse that it was too far from home.

Ron and I decided that once Jeff and Carol came to a Christian environment in America, things would be easier.

Finally, we said goodbye to Jeff and Carol with the promise that I would send airline tickets for them to have a vacation in America. Carol was to phone me from England to let me know how their plans were progressing. Naturally, we insisted on Jeff no longer contacting the spirit world. He promised us faithfully that he would cooperate on this matter.

Ron and I returned to America with mixed feelings. We were happy because we had witnessed for Jesus, but we were dissatisfied that Carol and Jeff had not yet given their hearts to Him. But, we felt, all was not lost.

After a week, Carol called collect from London to tell me that Jeff was having a struggle stopping himself from being controlled by demons. She said when he sensed the spirits around him, he would take his dog for a walk. I was extremely concerned and began to get very emotionally involved. I began to pray in a fashion that I had never done before. I shed tears in the privacy of my office and felt very burdened to be at this man's side. Financially this was impossible. I had no money and I was terribly frustrated.

Carol made some more calls from England and I sensed that things were not too good. I spoke about these problems to two church friends named Henry Doss and John Goodman and they offered me the money to return to England. I thanked them profusely.

I phoned Ron Sunseri in Oregon to tell him what had happened and that I was returning to England. He said, "Ben, I will meet you in Chicago. I am going with you." So once, again, armed with the gospel, we prepared to confront Satan. We were more determined than ever.

Jeff and Carol were overwhelmed that we would come back for them. Jesus uses people to reach others and Carol could not help but see, through us, how concerned Jesus was for their souls. That night in London we once more taught them from the gospel.

Suddenly, in the middle of teaching, Carol jumped out of her seat and said, "I want to be baptized right now!" Jeff followed her lead. Ron baptized Carol and I baptized Jeff. Words cannot express the emotions that we all felt that night. In our minds we felt the sweet victory found in Jesus.

This time Ron and I returned home to America thoroughly happy men. We looked forward with much anticipation to Carol and Jeff coming to live as new Christians in America. We were excited for them and all the possibilites of their new life. We were totally unprepared for the heartache and despair that the next six months would bring.

Jeff and Carol's arrival coincided with my son's emigration from England. Stewart arrived just one day before the Millers. Unfortunately, Stewart and Jeff never hit it off and, as we all lived in the same house, the atmosphere was terribly strained.

No matter what we tried to do to remedy matters, it never completely satisfied Jeff or Carol. They would request something, we would fulfill their need, and then they would complain and demand something else. My family endured the most unhappy six months of our lives. It was inconceivable that two people could be so demanding.

The situation deteriorated steadily and culminated with Jeff and Carol's return to London and spiritualism. A diary left by Jeff gave some clues to the reason for their unhappiness. Jeff had continued to contact the spirits after his baptism, and was still directed by them. One is reminded of the parable of the sower in Luke 8.

From that point on, I concentrated all my strength and effort on crusading against Satan's enticements and entrapments. I was determined to win back from the Evil One as many souls as possible who, like Jeff Miller, had fallen prey to his deceits.

7

LIVING IN THE LIGHT

Hopelessness is the only way I can describe my situation when I lived in London without Jesus. My search for knowledge about life after death brought me only misery and gloom.

One experience, in particular, represents my situation at that time. Jeff Miller was in trance and the spirit entity controlling him had given us details about reincarnation. The entity explained that the Hindus had the answer to life after death in *Samahdi,* a term meaning that after many reincarnations a person becomes perfect like God. There is an eternal bliss with NO SENSE OF ONE'S OWN EXISTENCE.

I complained, "having no sense of your own existence is just like being dead." The entity laughed at my dismay. I felt crushed and miserable. After being shown life after death, I was now being told there was a final death after all.

"What about these promises to live in a beautiful spirit world with our loved ones?" I asked. The spirit replied "That ceases and we no longer remember our past lives." The spirit then became vague and senseless in his answers, leaving me with an impression of hopelessness with death as the end product. The entity seemed to enjoy my perplexity and feeling of despair.

Devastated, I left the seance room. My life went from bad to worse. Satan knew what he was doing to me. He was destroying my soul. In John 8:44, Jesus said Satan is a liar, a destroyer and a murderer. In contrast, Jesus said of himself, "I am the light of the world; he who follows Me shall not walk in the darkness, but shall have the light of life," John 8:12.

Praise the Lord, I found the Light. The realization of that first taste of Christianity brought refreshing hope and chased away the darkness in my life. I discovered I was loved.

At the end of the first sermon I heard in that little church in Norwalk, California, people came over to me, shook my hand and told me how happy they were to have me in their church. No one had ever paid me that kind of attention before. I felt wanted, cared for. That's what won me to Christ. It is no wonder Jesus said, "A new commandment I give to you, that you love one another, even as I have loved you, that you also love one another. By this all men will know that you are My disciples, if you have love for one another," John 13:34, 35.

Excitement filled me. Surely if there was a spirit world of Satan, there was a spirit world of hope. There was another way of living, a way of light. The last twenty years of my life have been lived walking in that light.

Sure, the problems of life are still going on. The difference is Jesus walks through them with me. Peter said, "His divine power has given us everything we need for life and Godliness through our knowledge of Him who called us by His own glory and goodness. Through these He has given us His very great and precious promises, so that through them you may participate in the divine nature and escape the corruption in the world caused by evil desires" (II Peter 1:3, 4).

There was a time when my life was guided by signs and wonders. Jesus said, "Only an evil and adulterous generation seeks after a sign" (Matt. 12:39). Spiritualism was just one sign after another, it gave no peace. Today I accept Jesus on faith (Heb. 11:6). This is not a blind faith but faith in the facts of the Scriptures, faith in the facts of His death, and faith in the facts of His resurrection. No longer is the fear of death an obsession in my life. I have found eternal life in Jesus.

As Christians we know that heaven is real because the Holy Spirit dwells within us. He is the proof. As the Spirit lives within us, he produces "love, joy, peace, longsuffering, gentleness, goodness, faith, meekness and self-control" (Gal. 5:22-23). When we see these great spiritual ideals come to fruition in our lives, we know that we are experiencing a foretaste of what life is going to be in the presence of God, Himself. As the Holy Spirit generates spiritual life within us, as He gives us the strength to overcome temptation and sin, as He produces in our lives the qualities known as "the fruit of the Spirit" we have tangible proof that heaven is real.

SECTION II

WHAT YOU SHOULD KNOW ABOUT SPIRITUAL DARKNESS

8

THE WORLD OF SPIRITS

A. Spiritualism

Spiritualism is a religion the basic tenet and practice of which is conversing with the dead. According to the Spiritualism Manual of the National Spiritualism Association, "A Spiritualist is one who believes, as part of his or her religion, in the communication between this and the spirit world by means of mediumship, and who endeavors to mold his or her character and conduct in accordance with the highest teachings derived from such communion."

In 1974, I returned to Great Britain and went to the Spiritualists Association of Great Britain to speak to W. Hunter Macintosh, President. I explained to him that I had become a Christian and that it was against God's word to be a spiritualist. I remember saying to him, "Hunter, the Bible says there is a way that seems right . . . ." He stopped me and said, "Ben, don't tell me that there is a way that seems right unto man but the ends thereof are the ways of death,'" (Prov. 14:12). He quoted the Bible! He then went on to assert that theologians had twisted God's Word and that things were added to the Bible against Spiritualism.

The spiritualists get their teachings from the spirit world and it is frightening how these teachings are anti-Christ. Equally disturbing is the fact that when one goes to a spiritualist church he will find the same trappings as can be found in an ordinary church, i.e., pictures of Jesus, crosses, etc. Spiritualists read from the Bible except that, of course, they avoid reading the passages against spiritualism. They sing the very same hymns that Christians do. "Open my eyes that I may see" is one of their favorite hymns to open up a seance. They claim the 9 miraculous gifts of the Holy Spirit and even pray to Jesus asking for power. The spiritualist church comforts the sinner. It teaches there is no death, just a transition into the spirit world. If you lived a good life you will go to a very high plane where it is beautiful. If you lived an evil life then you will go to a gloomy plane but there is no need to worry because there are helpers in the spirit world who will come down and help you to reach a higher plane.

Spiritualists say there is no such thing as hell, judgment, or a devil to worry about and that as far as Jesus was concerned, he was only a medium of the highest order. The spiritualists teach that God loves unconditionally and no one is going to hell because it doesn't exist. Salvation is by works. The door to reformation is never, ever closed because there is always going to be help over on the other side!

Why People Try to Contact the Dead

I believe there are three reasons why people contact the dead: (1) the loss of a loved one, (2) the fear of death, (3) curiosity.

Can We Speak to the Dead?

There were certain times that God permitted the dead to return. We see an example of this in the account of the Mount of Transfiguration when Moses and Elijah appeared and spoke to Jesus. A second time we read about the dead returning is when Samuel returned to speak to King Saul (I Sam. 28). King Saul went to a spirit medium to receive a message. The message was that he and his family would be dead the next day. The issue here is not whether this was Samuel or a spirit impersonating him. It lies in what the Bible says about contacting the dead. In I Chronicles 10:13, we are shown that the main reason why King Saul died was because he contacted a spirit medium. The spirit medium becomes a substitute savior in the lives of people. In this case the spirit medium, the Witch of Endor, became a substitute savior for King Saul.

The Word of God speaks very little about life after death; however Ecclesiastes 9:5 says:

> For the living know they will die but the dead do not know anything nor have they any longer a reward for their memory is forgotten. Indeed their love, their hate, their zeal have already perished and they will no longer have a share in all that is done under the sun.

The Bible says that as far as the dead are concerned, life on this earth is finished. They are in a completely different state. The apostle Paul says to be absent from the body is to be present with the Lord. In Luke 16, an account of a rich man who was in torment in Hades and a beggar, named Lazarus, who was in paradise, we see that once a person dies he is either going to one place or the other. It is interesting that the rich man began to think of his brothers and asked Abraham if he would send the beggar down to help them, "for I have five brothers that he may warn them lest they also come to this place of torment." Abraham said, "They have Moses and the prophets, let them hear them." But he said, "No, Father Abraham, but if someone goes to them from the dead, they will repent." Abraham replied, "If they do not listen to Moses and the prophets, neither will they be persuaded if someone rises from the dead." You see, Jesus rose from the dead and today still men are not persuaded. I believe this passage shows spiritualists are not speaking to the dead.

To Whom Do the Spiritualists Speak?

If then, the spiritualists are not speaking to the dead, to whom are they speaking? There are many scriptures in the Bible which give us clues about this. Leviticus 20:27 says, "As for a man or a woman, if there is a medium or a spiritist among them, they shall surely be put to death; they shall be stoned with stones, their bloodguiltiness is upon them." Deuteronomy 18:10, 11 speaks about the different manifestations of Satan, including among them mediums or spirits who call up the dead. Then God says, "For whoever does these things is detestable to the Lord and because of the detestable things, the Lord your God will drive them out before you." The Hebrew word here translated "familiar spirit" means demons.

In Spiritualism, the medium goes into a trance and is taken over by a spirit, who is not a guide of the dead but a demon impersonating the dead.

Psychic Phenomena

There are several types of psychic phenomena but only two forms of mediumship: mental and physical. The most common forms of mental mediumship are clairvoyance and clairaudience. Clairvoyance is the ability to see the spirit world and clairaudience is the ability to hear the spirits speaking. These phenomena can only be seen and heard by the medium. Materialization is a form of physical mediumship.

Mental Mediumship: Satan has an uncanny knack of knowing many things about us as shown in Acts 16:16. A minister from Yucca Valley, California, was dumbfounded when a psychic whom he had never met or seen told him his I.D. number accurately. There was absolutely no possible explanation other than the supernatural. Acts 16:16 explains that these kinds of people are controlled by a spirit of divination.

At spiritualist meetings the medium will sometimes go straight to a person and tell him the full name of a dead relative, how the relative died and very intimate details about the individual and the dead person. It is no wonder people become convinced they are receiving messages from dead loved ones.

Psychometry: Psychometry is similar to clairvoyance except that an article is used that belongs to the person the medium is trying to contact, regardless whether the person is alive or dead.

People who attend psychometry meetings are usually most anxious to contact a missing loved one. They place an article on a tray and are very careful to make certain that it does not touch some one else's article as it might interfere with the vibrations the medium is trying to pick up from the alleged owner. The medium will take one of the articles and relay the thoughts and feelings which come to him. The people believe this is a spirit guide who supposedly is contacting the original owner of the article, whether he be dead or alive.

This method of contact has been popular with law enforcement. On very rare occasions, bodies of missing persons have been found. Because of this very fact many people become converted to spiritualism. They cannot imagine Satan ever doing anything except evil. These people don't realize that Satan comes as an angel of light (II Cor. 11:13, 14) to lure us to him.

Materialization: One of the most incredible facts about spiritualism is the frightening reality of raising the presumed spirits of the dead through a supernatural phenomenon known as materialization. This phenomenon is a proven scientific fact and was the main reason why I became an avowed spiritualist.

In *Webster's Third New International Dictionary,* the second definition given for ectoplasm is:

> (2) The emanation from a spiritualist medium that is believed to effect telekinesis and similar pheonomena.

The phenomenon of materialization is extremely dangerous and the medium's life is placed in danger. Actually a type of hemorrhaging takes place. Life blood oozes out of the medium in a very unusual form and solidifies as it hits the air. The ectoplasm builds up into a form that can walk around and even talk to the sitters all the while being attached to the medium by a thin strip. After a while the power seems to subside, and the spirit becomes formless again, eventually going back into the body of the medium.

The most convincing proof of life after death, as far as the spiritualist is concerned, is seen through the evidence of materialization. This is a method which enables the onlookers to either see, hear, or feel the spirits themselves. The medium, of course, is being used by the spirit entities to produce these results.

What actually happens is that ectoplasm is extracted from the onlookers in an invisible form. This is psychic energy. Ectoplasm is the life blood of a person. Without it a person could not exist. This substance is God's creation. Satan cannot create life, but he obviously can take creation (ectoplasm) from willing human victims in the seance room and form his own counterfeit creation. Satan is a supernatural being and creates supernatural phenomena (Exod. 7:11, 22; 8:7; Matt. 24:24; II Thess. 2:9-11; Rev. 16:14).

In the phenomenon of materialization Satan comes in the guise of a vampire, extracting the lifeblood of a person (ectoplasm) trespassing God's will (Lev. 20:27; Deut. 18:10), and lying (John 8:44) by implying the phenomenon is the raising of the dead. Unfortunately I was involved as an observer and a believer for many years before I found the truth about spiritualism.

It is extremely difficult for an outsider to gain admission to this kind of seance for two reasons:

(1) This type of medium is very rare.
(2) Most circles that are involved in the phenomenon of materialization do not divulge their existence because the medium's life is in danger.

However there are times when certain personalities are involved, as seen in the following paragraphs, for publicity purposes. These people unwittingly promote Satan. Evidence of demonic activity today is overwhelming. There are some extracts from competent witnesses who have been involved in materialization seances.

Raphael Gasson

Former spiritualist Raphael Gasson was an ectoplasmic medium. In his book *The Challenging Counterfeit,* he writes:

> During this sort of seance the operating spirits make use of a substance which is drawn from the medium's own body. This substance is a semi-luminous thick vapor which oozes from the medium's mouth, ears, nose, eyes, or from the stomach and is dimly visible in the gloom. This mist which gradually becomes solid, as it eventually makes contact with the natural surroundings of the seance room, is called *ectoplasm* and is the basis of physical phenomena.
>
> Ectoplasm being sensitive to light, necessitates the seance being conducted in darkness. Experiments have been made to produce ectoplasm in light with, however, only limited success. Nevertheless, photographs in darkness have been taken with special cameras and they present a very strange and repulsive sight, with the ectoplasm hanging down like icicles from the mouth, nose, etc., of the medium. When

touched (only permissible by the controlling guide) it will move back into the body and if suddenly seized the medium will scream out or be caused to be violently sick. Such sudden graspings of ectoplasm have very often caused great bodily harm to the medium and could even result in loss of life. The reason for this being so dangerous is that the ectoplasm becomes solid through contact with the air and before it is able to enter back into the medium's body in the normal way, it has to dematerialize to its original state. If touched suddenly, without warning or permission, or unexpectedly contacted with light, the solid ectoplasmic mass will rush straight back to the body of the medium before having a chance to dissolve to its natural state. I have known of many mediums who have been crippled or blinded for life owing to the sudden impact of the solid ectoplasm which springs back with as much force as if it were connected to the medium by an excessively strong piece of elastic. I myself was blinded for nearly 24 hours after such an incident occurred. The force of the ectoplasm against the stomach caused a scar from side to side, which took many days to disappear.*

Scientists

Sir William Crookes was honored with degrees from five universities. He was the inventor of the Crookes tube and the discoverer of Thallium. Sir William Crookes saw many materializations and subjected these manifestations to scientific tests to prove beyond a shadow of a doubt there were forces at work which could not be explained by physical law.

Another scientist, W. J. Crawford, B.Sc., of Belfast, a well known writer of scientific treatises, tells of his experiments in ectoplasm with a materialization medium by the name of Kathleen Goligher.

When spirits materialized she was placed on a weighing machine and lost several pounds. The onlookers were also weighed at the same time and lost a small portion of weight. On one occasion the medium lost 54-1/2 lbs. Nearly all the weight loss was recovered when the phenomena ceased.

When I was at seances of this type I felt cold. Other sitters have experienced the same coldness. The temperature in the room had not

---

* *The Challenging Counterfeit,* p. 74.

changed. This fact is another proof of Satan extracting the life force out of a person for his own needs.

Baptist Minister

Victor Ernest, a baptist minister from St. Paul, Minnesota, tells in his book *I Talked with Spirits* about how he became involved in Spiritualism because of the death of his sister.

His younger sister was a trumpet medium. This is a phenomenon where a cone-shaped instrument is placed in the center of the room. This trumpet is made of aluminum or plastic and is painted with luminous paint to enable it to be seen in the dark. The medium goes into trance and ectoplasm emanates from the medium. The ectoplasm becomes solid around the vocal cord of the spirit and ectoplasmic rods emanate from different parts of the medium. Grippers pick up the trumpet and voices are heard through the cone shaped instrument.

The following is an excerpt from Mr. Ernest's book.

> When the medium entered his trance, the trumpet rose slowly from the table and dipped into a horizontal position. Eerily, it began spinning with a soft whir and moved around the room, stopping at intervals in mid-air.
>
> I sat in amazement. I saw the floating trumpet, but I could not believe it. The residents of the home seemed to accept the experience as a very common thing.
>
> The trumpet went first to my mother and then to other members of our family. And we heard a voice, supposedly my departed sister's, but at first we could not distinguish the words.
>
> Then the trumpet came to me. My first reaction was to grab it, and I snatched at the mouthpiece, but it darted away with amazing swiftness. I tried again, but it moved faster than I did.*

Of these trumpets, Raphael Gasson, in his book *The Challenging Counterfeit,* said:

> At some of these seances mediums will use as many as four or five trumpets at once, all flying around in different directions without knocking against each other, all speaking in different voices at the

---

* I Talked With Spirits, pp. 16, 17.

same time, which does more or less prove the integrity of the medium, as he could hardly be speaking in four or five voices simultaneously.

Newspaper Reporter

"Cassandra" was the pen name for William Connors, a famous newspaper reporter for the largest publishing newspaper in the world, *The Daily Mirror* of Great Britain. He was well known for telling it like it is. He once interviewed the famous pianist Liberace. He reported his feelings about Liberace and *The Daily Mirror* had to settle out of court. Later Bill Connors was honored and knighted by the Queen of England for his forthright reporting.

Sir William Connors reluctantly went to a trumpet seance. He took along with him photographer Leon Isaacs. The article he wrote was illustrated by photograph with the following description beneath it: "The medium in a trance, lashed to the chair, while a table leaves the ground and books fly through the air . . . a photograph taken during the seance attended by 'Cassandra.'" The heading of the article was "'Cassandra' got a surprise at Seance," and his report, in his caustic manner, reads as follows:

I claim I can bring as much sceptism to bear on spiritualism as any newspaper writer living, and that a powerful load of sceptism these days. I haven't got an open mind on the subject—I'm a violent, prejudiced unbeliever with a limitless ability to leer at the unknown. At least, I was till last Saturday. And then I got a swift, sharp, ugly jolt that shook most of my pet sneers right out of their sockets.

Trumpets sprayed with luminous paint shot around the room like fishes in a tank. They hovered like pike in a stream, and then swam slowly about. The rough stertorous breathing of the medium continued, and a faint tapping sound heralded a voice speaking from one of the trumpets in a childish voice.

Suddenly a heavy table slowly left the ground. The man who was sitting next to it said calmly: "The table's gone!" The photographer released his flash—you see the result on the right.

At no time did I see the medium move from his chair. I swear it.

What price cynicism? What price heresy?

Don't ask me what it all means, but you can't tell me now that these strange and rather terrifying things don't happen.

I was there. I saw them. I went to scoff. But the laugh is sliding slowly round to the other side of my face.

(Signed) "Cassandra"

I know exactly what "Cassandra" means.

The Power Behind Spiritualism

The apostle Paul makes very clear the power behind Spiritualism. He writes in Ephesians 6:12, "For we are not contending against flesh and blood, but against the principalities, against the powers, against the world rulers of this present darkness, against the spiritual hosts of wickedness in the heavenly places." Paul tells us of real personalities in the spirit world trying to gain control of our minds.

Throughout the Bible we see demons controlling the lives of people. The Gadarene was controlled by a legion of demons. Jesus tells us in Matthew 12:43, of a spirit bringing seven more demons into a man. The girl in Acts 16:16 had a spirit of divination. Yes, there is a power.

But praise the Lord, there is a greater power: the person of the Holy Spirit. "He who is in you is greater than he who is in the world," I John 4:4. As Christians we do not have to be afraid of Satan (II Tim. 1:7).

> Then comes the end, when he delivers the kingdom to God the Father after destroying every rule and every authority and power (I Cor. 15:24).

> I have said this to you, that in me you may have peace. In the world you have tribulation; but be of good cheer, I have overcome the world (John 16:33).

B. *Prophecy (Fortune-Telling)*

The Bible warns us in Acts 16:16-18 to beware of fortune tellers.

> And it came to pass, as we went to prayer, a certain damsel possessed with a spirit of divination met us, which brought her masters much gain by soothsayng.

> The same followed Paul and us, and cried, saying, These men are the servants of the most high God, which shew unto us the way of salvation.

And this did she many days. But Paul being grieved, turned and said to the spirit, I command thee in the name of Jesus Christ to come out of her. And he came out the same hour.

From these same scriptures we learn several things:

1. It is possible for a person to have a spirit of divination. Divination means the art of obtaining secret information from the spirit world forbidden by God (Deut. 18:10).
2. She was able to tell the truth (Matt. 7:21).
3. Paul spoke to the spirit (not to the slave girl) and demanded it to come out of her. The spirit came out of the girl at that very moment.

In the twentieth century prognosticators are busier than ever. In the past several years I have spoken and listened to many of these self-proclaimed men and women of God.

Without exception, all of them claimed their messages came from a higher source or from God Himself. I am quite certain these people don't realize how serious and dangerous it is to call one's self a prophet of God. Obviously, any serious student of the Bible can see these self-proclaimed prophets know little or nothing concerning the Word of God on the matter of being a prophet of God. It is my sincere desire that they will closely study God's Word for themselves in this message.

First, let us examine the claims of the most outstanding prognosticator in America today.

Jeanne Dixon claims to be a prophet of God. She accurately foretold the assassination of Mahatma Ghandi, Martin Luther King and the Kennedy brothers, plus several others. Sometimes, however, her predictions are so vague that they could not possibly be wrong, much like astrological prophecies.

Worse than that, she is often ABSOLUTELY WRONG, but this doesn't get much publicity. She predicted Red China would go to war over Quemoy in 1958 and cause World War III. She conceded the 1968 Democratic presidential nomination to Lyndon Johnson, but Hubert Humphrey got it. She saw Russia making the first manned lunar landing. George McGovern she announced, would not be a 1972 presidential candidate.

Bible Condemns False Prophets

According to the Word of God, her inaccurate predictions put her life in a dangerous position. Deuteronomy 18:20 says prophecy given by God is always true. God cannot lie. If a person's prophecy does not come to pass that person has told a lie. Under the Old Testament, Jeanne Dixon would have been put to death because of her lying failures. Today, under the New Testament, this is a spiritual death unless she repents.

Can We Have Prophets Today?

The Word of God is clear concerning modern day prophets or psychics:

1. Hebrews 1:1-2—Explains the Word of God came in many different ways: dreams, visions, etc. However, today the Word of God comes through His Son, Jesus. John 1:1 reads, "In the beginning was the Word and the Word became flesh." Jesus is the living Word. The Bible is the Word.
2. II Peter 1:3—God tells us everything we need is through Jesus.
3. Matthew 6:30-32—Tells us heathens only worry about the future. We should put our trust in God.
4. Revelation 22:18—Nothing more is to be prophesied or added to God's Word.
5. Matthew 12:39—Jesus said only evil people look for signs and wonders.
6. Matthew 7:20—Jesus said, "Not everyone who calls me 'Lord, Lord' will enter into heaven, only those that do the will of my Father."

People who put their trust in modern day prophets (substitute saviors) do not put their trust in God. The Bible is clear prophecy ceased when we received the final completed Word of God which we now have today. True, these modern false prophets are sincere, but they are sincerely wrong.

Proverbs 14:12—"There is a way which seems right to a man, but its end is the way to death." Why go to psychic readers when we can go to God's Word—the Bible?

C. *Witchcraft*

In his *Screwtape Letters,* C. S. Lewis presents the following warning concerning the demonic:

There are two equal and opposite errors into which our race can fall about demons. One is to disbelieve in their existence. The other is to believe, and to feel an excessive and unhealthy interest in them. Satan would be equally pleased by both those who don't believe that witchcraft and demons exist today and those who practice this unholy forbidden art.

The writer is concerned with both parties, i.e., Christians who teach that witchcraft is fraud and does not exist today, and those involved in worshiping the devil. Both parties deny the teaching of God on this subject.

The term witchcraft has many meanings. Witchcraft conjures up in one's mind such things as magic, demons, the supernatural, drugs, sorcerers, fortune-tellers, voodooism, etc. Basically witchcraft is a mixture of superstition, immorality, lust, drugs, idol worship, satanism, and spiritualism. Witchcraft takes many forms, but it is anti-social. Many are encouraged into it purely with the promise of thrills.

Witchcraft in the Bible

The first occult explosion possibly began in the time of Moses. The children of Israel were preparing to enter into the promised land and Moses warned them not to follow after the customs of the nations living there. Moses said,

> When you enter into the land which the Lord your God gives you, you shall not learn to imitate the destestable things of those nations. There shall not be found among you anyone who makes his son or his daughter pass through the fire, one who uses divination, one who practices witchcraft, or one who interprets omens, or a sorcerer, or one who casts a spell, or a medium, or a spiritist, or one who calls up the dead. For whoever does these things is detestable to the Lord (Deut. 18:9-12).

First, God said, "There shall not be found among you anyone who makes his son or daughter to pass through the fire." Compare this with Deuteronomy 12:31. Orgies were held and as a result children were born. These children were tossed into the fire and burned alive in the belief that they belonged to the fire god Moloch.

Second, God forbids the use of divination. Divination, of course, means the art of obtaining information form the spirit world forbidden by God. Acts 16:16 is a classic case of divination. In this account there is a girl who had a spirit of divination, a demon, and was bringing her masters much profit by fortune-telling. Verse 17 suggests she was good at it. She knew who the apostle Paul was and told the truth about his mission. Despite this, Paul sent the demon out of her. Demons are real.

Third, interpreting omens is the next thing forbidden. This is interpreted as cloud watching and Moses here is referring to astrology. Isaiah 47:13 gives a stern warning to the Jewish nation not to get involved in astrology. The people were worshiping the creation rather than the creator.

Fourth, God speaks about sorcery. Sorcery is often mentioned in the Bible, and refers to the use of drugs. People were involved in drugs in those days just as they are now, cf. Galatians 5:20; Deuteronomy 18:10; Revelation 21:8, 22:15. The Greek word for sorcery is *pharmakeia,* the source of our word pharmacy.

Fifth, spirit mediums or spirits, or those who call up the dead are condemned by God. In I Samuel 28, we read that King Saul went to a spiritualist medium. He had been cut off from God and so he turned to spirit mediums. A seance took place and a spirit materialized. The Bible is very clear in I Chronicles 10:13, that King Saul died because he consulted a medium.

Conclusion about Witchcraft

The Bible makes divination, astrology, sorcery (drugs), and spiritism unacceptable in the Christian life. The Bible is clear; demons do exist. Their number and power are great, but "greater is He who is in you than he who is in the world," I John 4:4. "When He had disarmed the rulers and authorities, He made a public display of them, having triumphed over them through Him," Colossians 2:15.

D. Demon Possession

We are living in an age of phenomenal progress in the conquest of the universe. The danger of all this is that man's achievements are being worshiped. Science is proving natural law and at the same time scientists are trying to disprove the supernatural law of God. No wonder humanism is steadily creeping into the lives of the unbelievers. This new age of thought not only denies God, but also denies Satan. The devil is quite happy man thinks this way.

Many sincere Christians are skeptical about demons. These people believe in God and accept Jesus as their Saviour but refuse to believe demons exist today. Some say demons were superstitious, others say demons were allowed to control people in the times of the apostles only and do not exist today. It is the writer's intention to prove, according to the Bible, the reality of demons today.

Do Demons Exist?

Jesus believed in the devil and demons. Yet when the subject is mentioned now, many well meaning Christians refuse to believe that demons exist in this day of "enlightenment." On the contrary the Bible tells us demons are our enemies and they are trying to control the very thoughts of men. The apostle Paul said "For our struggle is not against flesh and blood [human beings], but against the rulers, against the authorities, against the powers of this dark world and against the spiritual forces of evil in the heavenly realms" (Eph. 6:12, NIV). Obviously Paul is speaking about evil entities. If they are not demons, what are they? The New Testament offers over-whelming evidence of Satan and his legions of demons. Demons are real personalities; they are the agents of Satan sent out on a specific mission to destroy men.

What are Demons?

The Bible is silent on the precise identity of demons. It does not tell us how they came into being. The best explanation of the identity of demons is that they are fallen angels. When Satan rebelled he drew with him a great number of celestial beings (Luke 10:18; II Peter 2:4; Jude 6). There is no doubt that the principal angel that sinned was Satan. He was a murderer and a sinner from the beginning (John 8:44). The apostle Paul describes Satan's power as an organized army, with Satan the command in chief (Eph. 6:12).

The New Testament describes demons as spirit beings that have personalities. Demons are spirits; they do not have flesh and bones (Luke 24:39). However they are capable of entering and controlling people and even animals (Mark 5:13). Demons are intelligent. They think, they speak, they act (Acts 19:15, 16) through spirit mediums. They are knowledgeable and could speak (Matt. 8:29; Mark 1:34; Luke 4:33, 35, 41). Demons can cause physical ailments. They could make a person blind and dumb (Matt. 12:22ff., 9:32).

The Bible gives us an idea of their nature:

1. opposed to Christ   Luke 4:33ff.
2. opposed to believers   Ephesians 6:12
3. follow a leader   Revelation 9:11
4. consciences are seared   I Timothy 4:11ff.
5. eternally doomed   Matthew 25:41

What Is Demon Possession?

Demon possession is a condition in which one or more evil spirits inhabit the body of a human being, and take complete control of their victim. My experience in spiritualism convinced me that demon possession took place within the will of the medium. This happened because there was a passive submission on the part of the medium to foreign intelligences, namely demons or evil spirits. Two scriptures clearly show how this happens, Acts 16:16-18 and Matthew 12:43-45.

When a person allows his will to be taken over by an evil spirit, his consciousness can be temporarily blotted out and he becomes a slave to the inhabiting demon. A spirit medium, with whom I was familiar, would go into a trance six times a day. The trance sessions lasted anywhere from thirty minutes to two hours at a time. In trance, there were times when he would feel depressed and melancholy; sometimes he would be spiteful and ferocious. Between the attacks he would look healthy and appear normal.

Demons and Spiritism

We must never make the mistake of thinking that demons are just fantasy or figments of people's imaginations. Demons are real. The

Bible strictly forbids God's people to deal with the spirit world (Deut. 18:10-12; Lev. 19:31; 20:6, 27; I Chron. 10:13, 14; II Kings 21:6; 23:24; Isa. 8:19, 20). God would not forbid us to deal with something that did not exist.

Spiritism deceives us by claiming to contact the dead; actually these contacts are with demons who are impersonating the dead. Those who practice such divinations are actually violating the first commandment given by God—"Thou shalt have no other gods before me" (Exod. 20:3)—and are encouraging demon activity. There is much danger inherent in such practices because of the resulting imbalance of the mind and soul when one allows demons to control his thoughts and actions.

Satan's Goal

Before my wife became a Christian, she too was a spiritualist. Miranda tape recorded a private seance in which a spirit medium had gone into a trance. A spirit had taken over the medium and she was speaking in a very masculine voice. At the end of the seance, the spirit, speaking through the medium, said to my wife, "Are there any questions?" Miranda replied that she was trying to be a medium and give messages to help comfort the bereaved. She was, however, disappointed that the spirits never took control of her vocal chords and spoke in their voice through her. The spirit replied, "Don't be stereotyped. You people on earth are mainly concerned that we in the spirit world take control of your vocal chords. This is the least important to us. In the spirit world we work on pure thought. When we can take control of your thoughts we can easily take control of your mind and then use your brain to relay our thoughts to people."

Jesus said, "As a man thinks, so is he." The apostle Paul tells us we are fighting against principalities and powers. We are warned not to contact the spirit world because it will take control of us and our thoughts. When it has control of the thoughts it has the mind, will, action and can give its message through a ouija board, medium, fortune teller, psychic, etc.

After speaking on a late-night radio program in Fort Wayne, Indiana, I received a letter from a man who related to me how he became fascinated with the ouija board and found that in time he could manipulate it himself. After some months, the board told him to get a pencil. The pencil formed words and automatic writing began. "My hell on earth had just begun," he said. He became obsessed with his communication with a particular spirit. He lost his family and his job; he is now considered to be mentally ill. This is only one example of the many people who are involved in such experiences.

Results of Demonic Involvement

Four things, especially, are a result of demonic involvement. When a person becomes involved in fortune telling, playing with ouija boards, or any occultism, (1) the first commandment "Thou shall have no other gods before me" is violated, (2) divination, the art of obtaining information from the spirit world, though forbidden, is practiced, (3) demon possession is encouraged, (4) the unbalancing of the mind becomes a possibility. Often when a person becomes involved in the occult, he becomes physically or emotionally exhausted. His health starts to fail; there is a sense of apathy and weariness of living. A person becomes totally unfit for the duties of life. The depression is only temporarily lifted by going to the ouija board, a spirit medium, or by a spirit medium going to his guide. As a person develops into a psychic medium his mental and moral nature become disordered. He discovers that while it was easy to open the mental door by which the mind could be invaded, it is difficult if not impossible to expel the invader and shut the door. I know from my own personal experience.

Spiritualism held an unholy fascination for me. I ran from one seance to another, looking for fresh mediums, new signs and wonders. The Spiritualist Association of Great Britain had a cafeteria in the basement of its building in Belgrave Square. Whenever I had any spare time I would head for the cafeteria to drink tea and talk with any spiritualist there.

Demon Possession and Mental Illness

Mental illness has often been mistaken for demon possession. This type of thinking can complicate the well-being of the mentally sick person. It is important that before making a judgment we understand something about this problem. O. Quentin Hyder, M.D., in his book, *The Christian Handbook of Psychiatry* writes:

> A psychotic often experiences perceptual disruptions such as delusions or hallucinations; that is, he may believe something which is not true, or he may hear voices or see things which are really not there. Much of his time is spent in a world of fantasy. His mental functioning is sometimes so impaired that it grossly interferes with his capacity to meet the ordinary demands of daily living. Mood, memory, and clear logical thinking are sometimes so severely affected that he becomes unable to take care of himself or behave appropriately in the company of others. At this stage, for mutual protection compulsory hospitalization becomes mandatory.
>
> He is apparently out of touch with reality, and he says and does things in a manner which betrays his separation from the real world in which he lives. This leads to inappropriate behavior. What he says and does reveal that he has a disorder of thinking. You can detect this by patiently listening to a psychotic talking for a few minutes without interruption. You will begin to realize that he does not stick to the subject (loss of goal-directed thought), his mind wanders (flight of ideas), he goes off on a tangent away from the first direction of his remarks (tengential), he "beats about the bush" and never comes to the point (circumferential), and it may become so bad that there seems to be no connection whatever between one statement and the next (loosening of associations). His general appearance is likely to be untidy in manner of dress. His behavior, attitude and even facial expression may strike you as being unusual or peculiar. He may have a compulsive ritual, usually some harmless sequence of little actions which he has to do repetitively. He may appear tense or restless, agitated and unable to sit still. He may speak very fast, wring his hands, pace up and down, and even cry. On the other hand he may seem to be very withdrawn, brooding, and unable or unwilling to communicate. In the extreme condition of catatonia he will be totally out of contact with his surroundings, possibly staring blankly into space and unresponsive to painful stimuli.

Christians can suffer from illness, organic and mental. God sometimes permits mental sickness to come into our lives but He also provides relief through the love of Christians who care and understand. Let us be careful not to label everything we see as demon possession.

Can Christians Be Demon Possessed?

The New Testament not only commands us to preach Christ, but also warns us about the enemies of our souls—demons. They are not to be taken lightly. However, Christians can be sidetracked into making demon exorcism a ministry. They become obsessed with trying to cast out demons. This practice is inconsistent with the Word of God. Over the past several years I have listened to exorcists calling every sin and sickness a demon. These so-called deliverance ministers go into church and tell Christians that if they have certain characteristics they are demon possessed. They call them to the front of the church and begin to cast out demons of cancer, demons of stomach ulcers, demons of diabetes, etc. Then they start attacking the demons of sins: lust, greed, gossip, lying, homosexuality, etc. This list is endless. Not content with demons of sins and sickness they begin to cast out demons of loneliness, poverty, depression. By the time the exorcist is finished almost every Christian in the church believes he has a demon.

The problem with this type of thinking is that the guilt of sin is removed from the person involved and the blame is placed on the demon. God holds us accountable and personally responsible for our sins (Matt. 15:19). Nowhere does the New Testament say that demon possession is the cause of sin. Neither is all sickness related to demon possession. Most illnesses have no relationship to demons whatsoever. We must avoid two extremes of thinking:

(1) disbelieving that demons exist,

(2) blaming demons for all sins and sicknesses.

The problem with the belief that Christians have demons seems to be with the interpretation of the scriptures. People are told since the Bible speaks of a spirit of cowardly fear, any deliverance of fear must be by casting out a demon of fear. However, in the same verse the spirit of fear is mentioned, the scripture also speaks of a spirit of power and love and self-control (II Tim. 1:7). The word spirit in many cases means an attitude or disposition. David spoke of a broken spirit (Ps. 51:17). Paul came with a gentle spirit (I Cor. 4:21). Peter spoke about the adorning of the heart with a quiet spirit (I Peter 3:4).

Deliverance

The casting out of demons from Christians is not only unscriptural but very dangerous. Many Christians today are suffering from psychological problems because some zealous person believed he had power to cast out a demon. One hears of deliverance ministers working for hours to cast out a demon. Their "victim" ends up emotionally and physically exhausted. In Acts 16, when Paul commanded a demon to leave "it came out that very hour." Jesus never took hours to cast out demons. He just said a word (Matt. 8:16, 32) and the demon was cast out. In my ministry, almost every week I counsel people who have been told by ministers of the deliverance ministry that they are possessed. It is sad and this foolishness brings Christianity into disrespect. Rather than spend time seeking demons, these people should seek to evangelize the lost. Instead of filling people's minds with demons, they would do far better to fill their minds with the love of Jesus.

Jesus defeated Satan by quoting the Word (Matt. 4). We, too, must take our stand on God's Word and resist Satan and his demons (James 4:7). Let us put on the whole armor of God (Eph. 6:12ff.). Demons may be attacking us, testing us, but never possessing us. "Greater is He that is in you than he that is in the world" (I John 4:4).

9

PSEUDO SCIENCE

A. *Extra Sensory Perception*

What is E.S.P.? Simply defined, ESP is a sense of perception without the use of recognized channels. Most people associate ESP with premonitions or telepathy. However parapsychologists and psychic researchers experiment with ESP through many psychic channels: prophecy, spiritism, psychometry, yoga, clairvoyance, occultism, witchcraft, demonism, astrology, necromancy, out of the body experiences, transcendental meditation, etc. While this article will deal primarily with only the "premonition" aspect of ESP it will be necessary to establish its association with other aspects of the occult so that Christians will recognize ESP for what it is—a dangerous occult practice.

ESP is Real

In *E.S.P. for the Millions,* author Smith suggests that ESP is experienced by the "high and the lowly, the rich and the poor, the obviously well educated and those who, often by their own account, had little formal schooling . . . . There is no evidence that it favors any class of people or any intellectual level." (*E.S.P. for the Millions,* Susy Smith, Los Angeles: Sherbourne Press.)

Henry W. Pierce, a former practicing psychologist who wrote about scientific developments for the *Pittsburgh-Post Gazette* wrote a book called *The Scientific Truth about ESP* in which he has documented numerous occasions of telepathy, precognition and clairvoyance. He mentions one experiment by a Dr. Joseph B. Rhine, formerly of Duke University. Using a deck of 25 cards, Dr. Rhine found that certain people were able to name, time and time again, the card another person was looking at; some people could give the order of the cards in the deck when they were not being looked at by anyone else; some people could predict what order the cards would fall in after being shuffled. (*The Scientific Truth about ESP,* Signet Books: New York.)

Edgar Cayce was an individual with outstanding psychic ability. He gave some 30,000 readings in which he correctly determined the sex of unborn infants, diagnosed cures for illnesses including cancer, epilepsy, diabetes, nervous disorders, arthritis, etc.

Other books that document psychic phenomena are *Demonology Past and Present* by Kurt Koch, *Demons in the World Today* by Merril Unger, *I talked with Spirits* by Victor Ernest and *The Challenging Counterfeit* by Raphael Gasson. (When I read Raphael Gasson's book I thought I was reading my life story.)

The searching and seeking for ESP comes under the Biblical name of divination. Deuteronomy 18:12 clearly warns against any participation in divination. Acts 16 clearly shows the reality of divination and God's attitude toward it.

All ESP Is Not Fraud

Certainly there are many frauds involved in ESP. However a person who assumes that all ESP is fraudulent is treading a dangerous path. Children who are taught all ESP is fraudulent can reason then that there is no harm in playing with ouija boards, holding seances, or going to fortune tellers. Matthew 7:15 warns us "Beware of false prophets who come in sheep's clothing but inwardly are ravenous wolves." Fraud or fact, any attempt at ESP is clearly against God's will.

The Danger in Getting Involved

Involvement in the occult is usually a progressive matter. My own introduction to the occult world was through a chance encounter. A passenger in the cab I was driving introduced me to the spiritualist's concept of life after death. I began visiting the Spiritualist's Association, reading books on the subject, talking with mediums and visiting seances. I was captivated and found it almost impossible to do my work as a taxi driver in London. Wherever I dropped off a fare, I would check in my *Psychic News* for the nearest medium and go to a seance. Spiritism was an unholy fascination that I couldn't live without. Dabbling in ESP will most likely lead to a similar progressive involvement with the occult world.

God is a spirit and we are made in His image. We can yield our spirit to God or the devil. ESP requires from an individual a passive submission to demonic spirits. The spirits take over and control the individual, and ESP becomes a frightening reality. The seeking of unusual power or knowledge by means of occult activities is an open invitation to the devil. By yielding to God we can have the Holy Spirit within us and then greater will be He that is in us than He that is in the world!

Bob Braziel, an experienced preacher in Indiana, shared the following account of a personal experience he had in this area:

A few years ago, I accompanied two other preachers, an elder and a high school teacher to a public session of the Spiritualist Church at Chesterfield, Indiana. My school teacher friend was writing his Master's thesis on spiritualism and had gone to Chesterfield many times before. However, none of the others had ever been to this type of meeting before.

As we drove over to the place (about 70 miles away), I remember we were all laughing and joking about the new and strange experience which was before us.

We were seated in the place which could probably seat about 150 people. There were about 75 there that night. A man passed around "billets" (small pieces of paper) and explained that we should write down our names, the name of a deceased person we would like to contact, along with three questions to ask that person. Soon he came and collected them and set the plate with the billets up front on the platform in plain sight of the audience.

Then, he blindfolded a lady "medium" with two black handkerchiefs. The man who had collected the billets, then held the basket of billets over to the side of the lady, about 30 inches away from her. She took one out, rubbed it and said, "Is there a Bob Braziel here?" (She pronounced my name exactly right. Most people don't.)

I wanted to "make contact" with Laura Jondahl, who was my Grandmother who had passed away in 1940. I placed only her name on the billet and not her relationship to me. I had written down the following questions to be asked of her:

1. Are you aware of the cause of your death? (cancer of the liver)
2. Were you aware of the cause of death of your youngest daughter? (cancer of the liver)
3. Do you know where your son J.B. was at the time of his death? (he was in prison in California)

After calling my name, the "medium" said, "I have someone there for you, Mr. Braziel . . . a Mrs. Laura Jondahl. I believe she is your Grandmother, is that correct?" I answered, "Yes, ma'am!" The medium replied, "She (my grandmother) says, 'Yes,' she is aware that she died of cancer of the liver, but other organs were involved also. She said 'Yes,' she is aware of the awful suffering Bess (her youngest daughter) went through and her eventual death came from cancer of the liver. Finally, she said 'Yes, I knew that J.B. died in prison and this has caused me much grief.'"

The "medium" went on to the next billet, but I was aware now that I was tampering with something that I should not be. I saw the power of Satan in a way that I had never seen it before and I was afraid. I just wanted to get away from that place as soon as I could.

As I was driving home that night, I promised the Lord that I would never knowingly get involved in this type of thing again. My advice to all Christians everywhere is to beware. "Resist the devil and he will flee from you."

B. *Life After Death*

Several years ago I held a meeting in Philomath, Oregon. At the question and answer time, a very distraught lady began asking questions concerning life after death. I realized from her questions that she had been involved in seances, a very extreme form of spiritism. After the meeting was over, the minister and I spoke to her privately. With tears running down her cheeks, she said, "Mr. Alexander, you have destroyed my whole life tonight. The only hope that I had you have destroyed." It seems that some time before, her daughter, age 9, had died of drowning. She could not bear the thought that she would never see this child again on this earth, and she resorted to going to a spirit medium. I explained to her that these mediums were trading on the dead. She wasn't getting in touch with her daughter but with demons impersonating the daughter. I also tried every way that I could to assure her that because of the tender age of her child, no doubt she was in heaven and they would be together again. If God forbade us from contacting the dead because it is evil, surely He wasn't going to send this little child to lead us into hell and damnation through a spirit medium.

Death is a reality and a fact of life, but this was not the wish of God. Unfortunately it was man's own doing as he rebelled against God. Praise God, He sent us a Saviour!

Trading on the Dead

The world's inability to cope with death without Jesus Christ was further impressed on me when I returned to England and went to the Spiritualist Association of Great Britain to explain to the leaders why I had become a Christian. As I walked through the revolving door to this beautiful building sitting among the embassies in Belgrave Square, London, England, there on the right hand side was the reception center. On the wall were the names of the many spirit mediums on duty for that day. The association has a membership of 26,000 people and more are continuously pouring in. These mediums, male or female, are people who are sensitive to non-physical forces and have given themselves through a passive submission to foreign intelligences known as demons. We read about this in the Old Testament in Leviticus 20:27. They are familiar spirits. The Hebrew word is *Ob* and it means a demon. Again in Acts 16:16, we see a slave girl that had a spirit of divination. In reality these mediums act as substitute saviors in the lives of these people. Note Paul's response to the girl.

Where Are the Dead?

I believe that Jesus took the lid off of heaven and hell in Luke 16 with the story of the rich man and the poor man, Lazarus. Their conditions in this life are touched first. The rich man was selfish and lived a notoriously pleasure-seeking life. The beggar, of course, was afflicted in body as well as being a pauper. He sat at the rich man's gate every day and was dependent on scraps for survival. The text says the dogs were more kind to him than the selfish rich man was. Then there is a sudden change. Both men died, were buried, and that was the end of their earthly life. Then Jesus begins to describe the next life and there is a contrast which is frightening. The rich man was in Hades, a place for the unsaved, and he was "in torment." I believe that this torment was one of intense pain of the mind and the spirit. God does not send anyone to Hades. Whoever goes there goes by his own free will and as a result of his own actions.

In contrast, the beggar was in a place of happiness. The rich man could see Lazarus and in his own intense pain called upon Abraham to send someone down to comfort him from his torments. Abraham denied the request saying the great gulf was fixed and there could be no crossing over. One can understand why there had to be a great gulf fixed.

I know that there is an evil spirit world from my own experiences but more importantly because God tells us that there is a spirit world. He also tells us we shouldn't contact it.

Out of the Body Experiences

Magazines and television, even Christian television, are reporting on out of the body experiences. There is a book called *Beyond and Back* by Ralph Wilkerson, pastor of a pentecostal church known as Melodyland in Anaheim, California. He writes about Christians taking round trips to heaven, coming back and telling us what is going on. I personally saw on television on the 700 Club a lady who said she died on the operating table, took a round trip, saw her pet poodle in heaven but was told the time wasn't right for her. We even hear of people who do not know Jesus saying they have had a round trip to heaven and come back. There is so much misguided information.

What happened to them is open to speculation but as Christians we do not need to be experts on the occult. We need to be experts on the Word of God. The Bible certainly doesn't tell us that it is appointed unto man once to die, to take a round trip and come back and tell what is going on. That you will find only in the second book of imaginations. The Bible is clear, "It is appointed unto man once to die and after that the judgment" (Heb. 9:27). Let's not be concerned with people's experiences but with thus saith the Lord.

Does the Bible speak about life after death? Most certainly. Especially does it speak for the Christian. The apostle Paul said to be absent from the body is to be present with the Lord (II Cor. 5:8). Jesus said,

> Let not your heart be troubled. Believe in God, believe also in me. In my father's house there are many dwelling places. If it were not so I would have told you for I go to prepare a place for you and if I go and prepare a place for you I will come again and receive you unto myself, that where I am there you may be also (John 14:1-6).

C. *Astrology*

A Heavenly Illusion

Astrology surely must be one of the most widely believed superstitions of our time. Over 40 million Americans trust in the stars. To help them solve their daily problems, these people have at their disposal 10,000 full-time and 175,000 part-time astrologers. In the U.S., astrology has become a big business, estimated at 200 million dollars a year.

There are literally thousands of books printed on astrology for all special interest groups: *Astrology for Everyday Living, Astrology for Teens, Astrology Made Practical, How to Find Your Mate through Astrology.* The list is endless.

The Bell Telephone Company of Indiana at one time introduced a gimmick to induce people to use the telephone. They made available a brochure which gave telephone numbers (according to birth dates) to call for horoscopes. The horoscopes were prepared by astrologer Jeanne Dixon.

Astrologers are fallible. Carroll Righter, the famous astrologer to the Hollywood stars, was asked to give his opinion on the marriage of

Zsa Zsa Gabor to the English actor, George Saunders. Carroll Righter said that according to their constellations the marriage was perfect. Actually it ended in divorce in just a few short months. Carroll Righter couldn't have been "wronger."

How Astrology Works

The Zodiac, or imaginary belt of the heaven, is divided into houses, each containing a different constellation. There are twelve divisions, each being equal. The different houses or signs are each governed by a planet. Astrologers believe that individuals inherit the personality of the sign under which they are born.

A horoscope (the Greek word is "hour watcher") is the chart of the positions of the planets in relationship to one another at the exact time of your birth. Astrologers believe that your personality and your future can be determined by where each planet in the heavens was the moment you came into the world. According to astrologers, your *fate* was then sealed and there is nothing you can do about it. Astrologers tell us that you can avoid bad days and take advantage of good ones.

Why People Get Involved

There are four contributing factors to involvement in astrology: (1) We are living in an age of widespread fear and anxiety. The world cannot provide security. People want to know what the future holds so they turn to cults, psychics, superstition and astrology. Cf. II Timothy 1:7. (2) This is a time of confusion. America has become a permissive nation. The climate created by massage parlors, porno outlets, X-rated movies and ungodly television programs has drawn man away from God. The Bible predicted that "the time will come when they will not endure sound doctrine; . . . and will turn away their ears from the truth, and will turn aside to myths" (II Tim. 4:3-4, ASV). This problem is arising all over America. Back in March, 1969, *Time* magazine stated: "Predictive astrology, like divination and occultism, generally tends to take hold in times of confusion, uncertainty, and breakdown of religious beliefs." (3) The established church has failed to go to the Bible for the answers. Rather than face the problems, religious leaders indulge in philosophical and semantic patter. The Bishop of Woolwich started this trend in England and began to secularize Christianity by preaching "God is dead." Since then the popular church has begun to preach the social gospel. The true message of God has been scorned and ridiculed. Instead of preaching the Bible as the Word of God it is proclaimed as a book of myths and folklore. According to the astrologer Constella, "Many of astrology's new converts are refugees from religion." This is not surprising. Man is made in the image of God. Man is a spirit being. He is either filled with the person of the Holy Spirit or with the thoughts of a man-made religion—astrology. (4) We are living in an age of depersonalization. People are being denied their individual character. They want to be important, to be somebody. They want to determine their own life, do their "own thing." If they will not accept Jesus Christ as Savior they turn to a substitute—the astrologer. What they don't understand is that the astrologer robs them of their self-confidence. A person is left with the impression that he is incapable of running his own life. This way of life violates the principle that Jesus laid down on the Sermon on the Mount.

Do not be anxious then, saying, "What shall we eat?" or, "What shall we drink?" or, "With what shall we clothe ourselves?" For all these things the Gentiles eagerly seek; for your heavenly Father knows that you need all these things. But seek first His kingdom, and His righteousness; and all these things shall be added to you. Therefore do not be anxious for tomorrow; for tomorrow will care for itself. Each day has enough trouble of its own (Matt. 6:31-34, ASV).

Astrology and the Bible

Many astrologers quote the Bible to prove their belief. They claim God ordained astrologers (wise-men) to announce the birth of Jesus. This statement cannot be true because God condemns astrology.

Actually Matthew two says that "wise men from the East came to Jerusalem" (Matt. 2:1, RSV). The original word was *magi*. This referred to a caste of men who were scientists. They were men well educated in the art of astronomy, not astrology. These men were obviously well versed in the scriptures and no doubt were honorable men chosen by God to announce the birth of Jesus.

A scripture that clearly condemns astrology is Isaiah 47:13:

> You are wearied with your many counsels,
> Let now the astrologers,
> Those who prophesy by the stars,
> Those who predict by the new moons,
> Stand up and save you from what will come upon you (ASV).

Isaiah states in no uncertain terms the fate of those who follow after astrologers. He pointed out that the astrologers couldn't help themselves, let alone anyone else.

Amos 5:25, 26, connects astrology to the sacrificing of children: "Did you present Me with sacrifices and grain offering in the wilderness for forty years, O house of Israel? You also carried along Sikkuth (Moloch) your king and Kiyyun (Saturn) your images, the star of your gods which you made for yourselves" (ASV). Amos told the people of Israel that God was disgusted with their form of worship, because in their hearts they were following after celestial gods.

In the New Testament, Stephen condemns Israel again for the worshiping of the creation instead of the creator.

> And at that time they made a calf and brought a sacrifice to the idol, and were rejoicing in the works of their hands. But God turned away and delivered them up to serve the host of heaven; as it is written in the book of the prophets, "It was not to Me that you offered victims and sacrifices forty years in the wilderness, was it, O house of Israel? (Acts 7:41-42, ASV).

Astrology and Science

Many people think of astrology as a science. They tend to confuse astrology with astronomy. We know astronomy is a bona fide science concerned with the science of the stars, planets and all other heavenly bodies. This study deals with the composition, motion, relative position, size, etc. of these heavenly bodies. A former president of the American Astronomical Society, along with eighteen Nobel Prize winners and 168 other scientists, in 1975, signed a statement challenging "the pretentious claims of astrological charlatans." The statement disclaimed any scientific basis for astrology (*Good News,* Vol. 18, No. 10, Sept. 11, 1975).

Why Astrology Is Wrong

1. The Bible condemns astrology as evil. Deuteronomy 4:19; 17:3; II Kings 17:16; 21:3, 5; II Chronicles 33:3, 5; Isaiah 47:13; Jeremiah 8:2; 19:13; Daniel 1:20; 2:2, 10, 27; 4:7; 5:7, 8; Zephaniah 1:5; Acts 7:42, 43. There is a tendency among Christians to make light of astrology. This can be dangerous. One does not joke with what God denounces. It is a personal affront to our Lord, and shows spiritual ignorance.

2. Believers in astrology worship the creation rather than the creator. Romans 1:20, 21 says,

> For since the creation of the world His invisible attributes, His eternal power and divine nature, have been clearly seen, being understood through what has been made, so that they are without excuse. For even though they knew God, they did not honor Him as God, or give thanks; but they became futile in their speculations, and their foolish heart was darkened.

3. Astrologers are often innaccurate.

4. Astrology is unscientific and is condemned by true men of science—astronomers. Also other planets have been discovered since the zodiac was established (Uranus, 1781; Neptune, 1839; Pluto, 1932).

5. Astrology has been known to be fraudulent. Newspaper editors have used old horoscopes.

6. The power of suggestion plays an important part in astrology. Very often horoscopes (good and bad) come true because the reader makes them a self-fulfilled prophecy. Also, autosuggestion plays a very important role in astrology.

Astrology - Faith in Fate

Today, many are attempting to go beyond the faith that was once delivered to the saints. They do not trust God and look for a convenient way out. Astrology becomes a cop out for these people. They reject the living God and turn to a lying spirit. The writer of this article, who was once a spiritualist, remembers how strongly astrology is encouraged in spiritualism.

The Babylonians trusted in astrology several thousand years ago. Over forty million Americans trust in the stars in this modern twentieth century. God only honors those who trust in Him.

D. *Hypnosis*

Definition: The following definition is given for the term hypnosis: "A state that resembles normal sleep, but is induced by the hypnotizer whose suggestions are readily accepted by the subject."

To describe how or even why hypnotism works is extremely difficult. Even professional hypnotists from the medical field are not sure what happens. Perhaps a simple example would be that when you are alert and wide awake, your conscious mind can concentrate on present problems; you are aware of your surroundings. But sometimes part of the conscious mind wanders off in a day-dream; you lose your sharp awareness and when a friend asks a question, you fail to hear. This state of absentmindedness is somewhat like a form of hypnosis.

Hypnosis and Medicine

In the medical profession some doctors and psychologists use it to help certain patients (it does not work on everyone). The idea is to distract the patient's conscious awareness so that the hypnotist can talk with deeper levels of the mind. When a patient is submissive to hypnosis, he goes into a trance-like state, and is only aware of the hypnotist and his suggestions. In some cases hypnotism does help emotionally disturbed people who have buried or forgotten some painful event of the past. The hypnotist helps him to recall the event without the painful memory. Often such a patient sees his buried emotions in a new light and recovers.

Hypnotism can also be used to numb pain, especially when a patient may be unable to stand an anesthetic. Hypnotism seemingly can be very useful in the field of medicine BUT THERE ARE DANGERS!

Hypnosis and Dentistry

Among several letters that I have received in the past concerning hypnosis I quote the following:

Doreen was a brilliant student in high school, often on the honor roll. She was self taught on the piano and played classical music very well. After high school she got a receptionist job for the local dentist. She worked there for about two years. She broke the news to her folks that she was the subject of an experiment for the doctor that she worked for and his doctor friend. They had assured her that no harm would befall her. The experiments entailed a considerable amount of hypnosis. Gradually her personality changed. She is now considered a split personality.

The remainder of the letter is very sad indeed. This young brilliant girl was admitted to a mental hospital, had several electric shock treatments. She is under heavy sedation constantly. Her parents have spent money on many doctors. Many times her parents have awakened in the early hours of the morning to find her sitting in a rocking chair, wringing her hands and crying. When they talked to her she said "the voices" told her that they would do harm to her mother and sister if she did not take notice of what they said. She lives at home, seldom speaks, and is grossly overweight.

Hypnosis and Reincarnation

Several years ago in Springfield, Missouri, Burt Ward, minister of the Southland Christian Church, and my wife and I were watching an intriguing news item on television. A minister's wife was being hypnotized for the relief of back trouble. To the surprise of everyone, this lady was speaking fluently in a foreign language. The television station arranged to bring in the services of a linguist, especially when they found out that the hypnotized lady had never even learned another language, and had never been outside America. The lady was hypnotized and a conversation took place between the linguist and the lady concerned. The linguist said that the language was 17th century German, and that the personality speaking through the hypnotized lady claimed to be a girl who died in the 17th century and was using this lady's body as a process of her reincarnation.

Hypnosis Brings Out Psychic Abilities

Stanley Mitchell, President of the International Guild of Hypnotists, claims that he has hypnotized more than 20,000 people over the past

34 years. He discovered that while under hypnosis some people *spontaneously* demonstrated the abilities of clairvoyance, precognition and mind reading. He said that "perhaps the strangest case of all was that of a woman who suddenly showed real signs of distress under hypnosis. When I awakened her she said that a dear friend in another state had been taken to the hospital and was seriously ill. She was so distressed that I had her telephone. She was told that her friend had suffered a ruptured appendix just hours before and was in critical condition at the hospital. This friend died two days later." Dr. Harold Crasilneck, a Dallas psychologist and past president of the Society for Clinical and Experimental Hypnosis, said, "Persons under hypnosis can react to suggestions even before the hypnotist has had time to utter them." He went on to say, "I have worked with patients who anticipated what I was going to tell them to do."

"Hypnosis enhances a patient's psychic ability on occasion, and it happens far more frequently than many clinical hypnotherapists will admit," said Dr. David Cheek, a San Francisco obstetrician, gynecologist and clinical hypnotherapist. "I have run into this kind of thing frequently—hypnosis brings out E.S.P. in people who ordinarily would not exhibit it. It is undoubtedly true that hypnosis frequently brings people's latent psychic talents to the surface."

Christian Minister Speaks to Spirit

A well-known Bible professor of one of our Christian colleges tells of a bizzare incident while visiting a Christian Church. The minister told the professor that he used hypnosis when counseling. One of his subjects was a young lady who, while under the hypnotic trance, spoke in a masculine voice. Several of the members recognized the voice of a dead elder. The dead elder then gave them advice on how to run the church. The professor found this difficult to believe. He was invited to one of these hypnotic counseling sessions; the young lady was put into a trance and proceeded to speak in a masculine voice and asked the professor if he wished to speak to anyone. The professor answered "Yes," requesting to speak to his father who had been dead for about two years at that time. It was the intention of the professor to expose this whole thing as a fake. Instead the professor had a shock when he asked three questions to which no one but a member of the family would have known the answer. Not only did he get the correct answer each time, but it was in the very phraseology that his father would have used when he was alive. He went home, studied his Bible and found many Scriptures concerning the occult, witchcraft, divination, familiar spirits, demons, etc. He sent these to the minister who in return said that he caught the spirit in some lies, and had given the practice up.

Hypnosis and Spiritism

In an article in *Cornerstone* magazine, Rabindranath Maharaj, author of *Death of a Guru,* has said that when an individual's mind is in a passive state (by means of drugs, hypnosis, meditation, etc.) his spirit is cut off from his brain. This allows a demon to control his mind. Rabi also referred to Sir John Eccles, noted authority on the brain. Sir John commented that "the human brain is a machine that any ghost could operate."

Once a person allows himself to be under the spell of a hypnotist, his brain is cut off from his own mind, and taken over by another source. In the case of the medium, because there is a passive submission on the part of the medium to these foreign intelligences, he becomes demon possessed.

Dr. Paul Tournier, a famous physician in Geneva, states that every form of hypnosis is an invasion into the personality of man.

Hypnosis undermines the will, weakens it and prepares the way for intrusion by demons. One cannot be hypnotized for purposes of healing or anything else without subjecting the mind to somebody else. This is in opposition to God's Word which tells us that we should have the mind of Christ at all times (Phil. 2:5). Hypnosis also violates a fruit of the Spirit, self-control (Gal. 5:23).

Hypnosis is based on a submission to supine authority. It is like the spirit of angel worship forbidden by God (Col. 2:18). Hypnosis is nothing new. It has been used by Hindu Fakers, voodooists, magicians, sorcerers and spirit mediums. In *Strong's Concordance,* the Hebrew word for charmers is *cheber,* to cast a spell. There is a possibility this could be associated with hypnosis and forbidden by God in Deuteronomy 18:10.

No man can serve two masters (Matt. 6:24). Our minds and our wills should be subject only to God. "You shall worship the Lord your God and serve Him only" (Luke 4:8). Also, "You shall love the Lord your God with all your heart and with all your soul and with all your *mind*." To surrender one's mind or will to anyone other than God is therefore a sin against God and a subversion of true religion.

✝

10

EASTERN MYSTICISM

It is difficult to understand how in this scientific age of ours thousands of young people in the United States are abandoning Christianity in exchange for the proven failure of Eastern mysticism. It is unbelievable that these young people are willing to listen to Eastern gurus whose philosophy has only brought despair in a country which thinks more of its well fed cows, and allows rats to eat off the land while millions of its own children are starving.

Why are our young people turning East? I believe that there is a cry of desperation; a longing to be wanted. As I travel the country I see a cry for help among these young lives, who are seeking for a purpose to life. There are several reasons why they have turned to the East.

1. The young people are looking for human friendship, warmth, and affection instead of loneliness and alienation from their fellow man.
2. They are looking for a way to experience life and God more directly.

3. They are wanting an authority, a father-like figure. That is why Jim Jones was accepted. In the case of the Eastern turners they accept the guru.
4. They think that Eastern religions are not tainted by money and power structures.
5. Some are drawn to this Eastern philosophy for health reasons.
6. There is a devotion to a deity.
7. There is a desire for the tranquility of meditation.
8. There is a search for an inner peace.

When one examines this list of goals, it quickly becomes evident that those who are involved in Eastern mysticism are no different from anyone else. Most people in America today are looking for the same ideals. All that has happened is that these people have chosen a more dramatic way. These goals seem good and contain elements of truth. But when one carefully examines the numerous Eastern religions being offered today, there are obvious discrepancies. In Eastern religions *sin* is never mentioned, nor is *atonement* for sin considered necessary, because it is taught that man's nature is divine, and that the ultimate purpose in all human existence is the realization of this divinity within one's self.

The Eastern religions reject Jesus as Savior, therefore they are without the benefit of God's revelation. The best that they can offer is some kind of philosophy to be reconciled to. If that does not work, then they are promised that it will in the next reincarnation. The goal of the Eastern mystic is known as Samahdi—the highest attainable earthly state. In other words they try to annihilate their individual self into the impersonal essence of the Universe.

A. *Yoga*

One of the most subtle forms of Eastern religions being unwittingly practiced by thousands of Americans today is *Yoga*. According to Webster's dictionary, Yoga is:

1. Strict spiritual discipline practiced to gain control over forces of one's own being, to gain occult powers, but chiefly to attain union with the Deity of Universal Spirit.

144

2. A Far Eastern and Hindu Indian system of philosophy and psychology.
3. Mystical union with the Universal Spirit.

Many who practice Yoga think that it is a harmless exercise. This is far from the truth. Here is a list of statements the yogis believe:

1. Every bodily organ is related to the soul.
2. Every person has a physical and spiritual nature which strive with one another for pre-eminence. A harmony and union of these two natures is to be achieved through psychological exercises.
3. Man's eternal self is omnipotent, omnipresent and omniscient.
4. Man's eternal self is both *transcendent* and *immanent*. It is without end, having neither birth nor death. In essence *man* is *god*.
5. Heaven and Hell are products of man's mind.

Most systems of Yoga can be divided into three stages, at least for the Western mind. (There are actually seven stages of Yoga.)

1. First Stage: exercises and meditation.
2. Second Stage: control of body functions.
3. Third Stage: this stage of Yoga is nothing more than pure Spiritualism. You will find that the yogis are involved in materialization, this is where spirits literally solidify. They are involved in telekinesis, which is the moving of objects through an energy force. They are involved in states of trance, especially astral or soul travel. There is an organization called "Eckankar" who through special exercises is able to do this soul travel or out of the body experience. This is an extremely dangerous yoga practice.

The exercises in Yoga concentrated around the navel produce a general sensitivity. The exercises concentrated around the spleen (in which the Eckankar people specialize) relate to comprehension which leads to out of the body soul travel experiences. The exercises around the heart help the psychic vibrations. The exercises concerning the throat produce what is known as clairaudiance, and these exercises, when a psychic goes into trance, will enable a spirit to take control of a psychic's voice and use his voice. Other exercises have to do with the third eye. This is clairvoyance, where eventually a yoga practitioner will be able to see a spirit world of demons very clearly. The exercises concentrated on the cerebrum have to do with continuity of consciousness. The yogis believe that these exercises that they are doing are for the purification of the soul; but in reality they are helping them more and more to attain demon power.

Yoga Induces Psychic Power

Sometime ago I received a phone call from a Christian brother who was concerned about his daughter. She went to Humboldt State University and took a class on Yoga. Her problem was every time that they prayed at meal time she would give off the most piercing, terrifying scream. She had become psychic and could read people's minds; she explained this only took place after her involvement in Yoga. Fortunately this girl began to have a close walk with Jesus and never returned to the practice of Yoga.

Yoga Writers Sound Warnings

It is interesting to observe that pro-Yoga books warn of the possibilities of developing psychic power.
Guide to Yoga Meditation by Richard Hittleman.

Page 98—"There are great mental and physical forces within us which lie dormant; which are not being used. The practice of Yoga awakens these forces and as this occurs, the ordinary mind, our usual consciousness, is expanded."

Page 99—"I should like to state that I am aware of many, many people who began their study of Yoga strictly for the benefit which could be derived from the physical exercises and became deeply immersed in the philosophical pursuits as the *exercises began to arouse dormant forces!*"

Page 101—"Kundalini or basic power—when stimulated and aroused, the basic power makes an ascending journey up through the cord within the spinal column and according to how far it is made to rise, activates and opens, partially or fully, the various centers. These centers then begin to 'work' the areas of force in different parts of the organism over which they have control, are also awakened and their great storehouse of life-force is made available. This increased life force working within the organism helps to produce the expansion of consciousness.

It is through the gradual awakening and control of the centers that Yogis derive what is often referred to as *'supernatural powers'* and *'extra-sensory perception.'''*

Yoga Anti-Christ

Yoga is anti-Christ, and here are six reasons why:

1. It believes in re-incarnation (Heb. 9:27).
2. Yogis worship Hindu gods (first commandment).
3. Yogis worship idols (first commandment).
4. Self-realization (Eph. 2:8).
5. Harmony of our physical and spiritual nature is achieved through special exercises. (Divination, forbidden by God.)
6. Man is omnipotent, omnipresent, omniscient.

While I feel that it is not necessary to go into an indepth study of Eastern Mysticism, I do feel that it is essential for our children to understand and realize that these eastern cults do exist—they should be made aware of this fact. There is, of course, no need for them to become experts in Eastern Mysticism, or experts in the occult, but we do need our children to become experts in the Word of God.

B. *Transcendental Meditation*

The Founder

The founder of this movement was a man by the name of Maharishi Mahesh Yogi. Maharishi means a great sage. Mahesh is the family name and Yogi means a master of yoga. The very fact that at the end of his name he attaches the word Yogi means a teacher and practicer of yoga. A yogi will teach nothing less than yoga itself and although yoga itself is not a religion, it is a religious practice.

In his book *Meditations of Maharishi Mahesh Yogi,* pp. 17, 18, the Maharishi said:

> We do something here according to Vedic rites, particular, specific chanting to produce an effect in some other world, draw the attention of those higher beings or gods living there. The entire knowledge of the mantras of hymns of the Vedas is devoted to man's connection,

to man's communication with the higher beings in different strata of creation.

The Maharishi, by this statement, is telling us that T. M. is a religious practice. On page 95 of the same book, he says meditation is

a very good form of prayer. A most refined and most powerful form of prayer is this meditation which directly leads us to the field of the Creator, to the sources of Creation, to the field of God.

It is worth noting that when Jesus taught his disciples to pray he did not find it necessary to mention meditation nor did he assign them individual mantras.

Many people think that T. M. is harmless but it isn't. T. M. does not deal with sin nor does it advocate devotion to God. T. M. says that peace is attainable without a savior, that the source of the power lies not in a personal god but in man's heart. According to God man's heart is deceitful and desperately wicked. Paul said "beware lest any man spoil you through philosophy and vain deceit."

C. *Reincarnation*

Reincarnation is the belief of the Hindu religion that the soul re-appears after death in another and different bodily form. The process is believed to be repeated thousands of times until perfection is reached. This theory is very attractive to the sinner. He feels much safer believing the theory of reincarnation than believing the Bible—"the soul that sinneth, it shall die."

Reincarnationists believe that man's eternal self is omnipotent, omnipresent, and omniscient. They also believe that man's eternal self is both transcendent and immanent, that is, without beginning and without end, having neither birth nor death. They believe that man himself is a God.

Hypnotism's Proofs

The strongest so-called proofs of reincarnation are those produced by hypnotists. They claim that under hypnotic spells people are able to give facts about previous lives.

Hypnotism is being extensively used in spiritualism. Many spiritists are put into trance and different voices, supposedly from the dead, speak through them.

The Bible has the answer to this theory of spiritualism. In Jude 6 we read: "The angels which kept not their first estate but left their own habitation He (God) hath reserved in everlasting chains under darkness unto the judgment of the great day." II Peter 2:4 says, "God spared not the angels when they sinned, but cast them down to hell, and committed them to pits of darkness, to be reserved unto judgment." The Greek word, *tartaroo,* means to incarcerate. Jude and Peter indicate that certain angels sinned and that they are in darkness. In Ephesians 6:12, Paul says, "for we wrestle not against flesh and blood, but against principalities and powers and the rulers of darkness of this world and in spiritual wickedness in high places."

The Bible is clear that it is not a reincarnation process that is taking place, but a process of spirits taking over people's minds.

Reincarnation and the Seance

At one seance I attended I anxiously asked the "spirit" in control of the medium what was the final result of reincarnation. I was shocked at the answer I received. The spirit, speaking through the medium, said everything becomes peace. We become a light and are caught up into the Great White Spirit.

I asked the spirit again, "But what happens to our soul? Our way of thinking? What are we like? Do we see our loved ones? What will it be like?" The spirit seemed to enjoy my concern and my consternation and said again, "You are at peace and you don't think of anything. Your mind no longer exists. It's just at peace and that's it."

The spirit emphasized that all consciousness was finished. Life itself was meaningless. I was left with the impression of a kind of death, a vacuum, a complete hopelessness, thousands and thousands and thousands of years going forward to a complete blank. I think this was the most disappointing thing that I'd ever heard in spiritualism, and it left my spirit completely broken. Believe it or not, this is what millions of reincarnationists are working towards.

Jesus Contradicted the Reincarnation Theory

In Matthew 25:46, Jesus said, "And these shall go away into eternal punishment: but the righteous into eternal life." We do not keep returning until we are perfect. Hebrews 9:27 says, "It is appointed unto men once to die, and after this cometh judgment." The Bible is the final authority.

D. *Karate*

Should Christians participate in Karate? The writer of this article is of the opinion that Karate is a subtle weapon of Satan. John 8:44 tells us that Satan is a destroyer and it is my prayer that you carefully study the cunning nature of Satan in getting our youth involved in the use of Karate.

Karate and Christ

I have spoken to a number of Christians who have been involved in Karate and among them I find those who have been encouraged to practice meditation techniques and also Yoga—along with Karate lessons. Some of these brothers quit Karate because they realized that the more involved they became in Karate they experienced occult manifestation.

On the other hand, I have also spoken to Christians who do not use Yoga but do admit to a type of meditation technique. They feel it is in no way involved in the occult.

They also explain they go to schools to demonstrate Karate and this gives them an opportunity to witness for Christ. I will always praise God and say Amen that they witness for Christ. But the problem we have is that they have witnessed for Karate as well. The danger we have is that we have opened the door for possibly thousands of souls to enter into the occult which can only lead to final damnation. Christians advocating Karate must ask themselves: "Am I a stumbling block to a weaker brother?" (Rom. 14:1).

Even though one may participate in Karate without offending his own conscience he must consider the conscience of another who does not have the same knowledge of the danger involved. This consideration must be given because the weaker brother in Karate who may be practicing Yoga and deep meditation, etc. will be justifying his actions because the strong Christian participates. These opinions are going to be formed in the minds of the non-Christian teenagers in schools after watching and listening to Christians who advocate "Karate for Christ."

Christian leaders, please understand that *Yoga, I-Ching, The Chi* and *Meditation Techniques* are evil influences that can lead to disaster.

Remember it is not Karate that wins people to Christ. It can possibly have the opposite effect. Rather, it is the foolishness of preaching that wins people to Christ. Peter tells us that Satan goes about "like a roaring lion seeking whom he may devour" (I Peter 5:8). A lion only roars when it is too late for the victim to escape.

11

SPIRITUALISM IN THE CULTS

A. *Mormon Necromancy*

Webster's dictionary gives two definitions of the word *necromancy:* (1) the practice of claiming to foretell the future by alleged communication with the dead, (2) black magic sorcery.

The purpose of this message is to honestly present and document evidence that is not generally known among members of the Mormon Church concerning communication with the dead. My concern for my Mormon friends is the specific teaching of baptizing for the dead and consulting with the dead. I would ask my Mormon friends to compare God's holy word, the Bible, with the Mormon teaching of communicating with the dead. For many years I was involved in spiritualism (consulting with the dead). When I became a Christian I was shocked to find that this practice is strongly condemned in the Bible. Contacting the dead is viewed by God as flagrant apostasy and as a crime punishable by the severest penalties (Deut. 18:10-11; Lev. 19:31; 20:6; II Chron. 8:19-20).

Spiritualism in the Mormon Temple

The Mormon apostle Charles W. Penrose, said the ideal place to hear from the dead is in a Mormon temple. He said:

> The living are thus authorized, under prescribed conditions, to act for the dead. . . .
> This glorious doctrine bears the key to the sphere within the vail. It regulates the communion of the living with the dead. It saves those who receive it from improper and deceptive spirit communications. . . . Knowledge that is needful concerning the spiritual sphere will come through an appointed channel and in the appointed place. The *temple* where the ordinances can be administered for the dead *is the place to hear from the dead.* The Priesthood in the flesh, when it is necessary, will receive communications from the Priesthood behind the vail. (*"Mormon" Doctrine—Plain and Simple, or Leaves from the Tree of Life,* by Charles W. Penrose, Salt Lake City, 1897, pp. 51-52).

Mormons do admit and acknowledge that their leaders have contacted the dead. Joseph Smith was supposed to have been visited by a host of individuals, including John the Baptist, Peter, James, John, Moses, Elijah, Elias, Michael, Nephi, Moroni, Mormon and many others. On February 9, 1843, Joseph Smith gave a revelation telling how good spirits can be distinguished from bad spirits. It is now published as section 129 of the Docrine and Covenants.

Among other testimonies concerning contacting the dead, President Woodruff, fourth President of the Mormon Church, revealed: "I have had interviews with Brother Joseph until the last 15 or 20 years of my life. . . . I had many interviews with President Young, and with Heber C. Kimball, and Geo. A. Smith, and Jedediah M. Grant, and many others who are dead. They attended our conferences, they attended our meetings." (*Journal of Discourses,* Vol. 21, pp. 317-318)

President Woodruff claimed to have been visited by the signers of the Declaration of Independence:

> The dead will be after you, they will seek after you as they have after us in St. George. They called upon us, knowing that we held the keys and power to redeem them.
> I will here say, before closing, that two weeks before I left St. George, the spirits of the dead gathered around me, wanting to know why we did not redeem them. Said they, "You have had the use of the Endowment House for a number of years, and yet nothing has ever been

done for us. We laid the foundation of the government you now enjoy, and we never apostatized from it, but we remained true to it and were faithful to God." These were the signers of the Declaration of Independence, and they waited on me for two days and two nights. . . . I straightway went into the baptismal font and called upon brother McCallister to baptize me for the signers of the Declaration of Independence, and fifty other eminent men, making one hundred in all, including John Wesley, Columbus, and others; I then baptized him for every President of the United States, except three; and when their cause is just, somebody will do the work for them. (*Ibid.*, Vol. 19, p. 229)

Another Mormon who advocated speaking to the dead was the apostle Parley P. Pratt. He remarked:

A quarter of a century since, an obscure boy and his few associates, in the western wilds of New York, commenced to hold converse with the dead. Now, vision, new revelation, clairvoyance, mediums, oracles, etc., are talked of and advocated as far as the modern press extends its influence, or steam its power of locomotion.

An important point is gained, a victory won, and a countless host of opposing powers vanquished, on one of the leading or fundamental truths of "Mormon" philosophy, viz.—"*That the living may hear from the dead.*" . . . all the most holy conversations and correspondence with God, angels, and spirits, shall be had only in the sanctuary of His holy Temple on the earth, when prepared for that purpose by His Saints; (*Ibid.*, Vol. 2, pp. 45-46)

B. *Unity School of Christianity*

The Unity School of Christianity has a membership of 1,200,000 and is the largest gnostic cult in Christendom. They teach a system of belief combining ideas derived from Greek philosophy, oriental mysticism and ultimately, Christianity and stress a salvation available through positive knowledge in spiritual matters. In short, Unity believes you are your own judge and logically thinking, by being a good person you become a Christ-like person.

Unity teaches the beauty of living a good life. On the surface, just like its palatial headquarters, that seems beautiful. But then doesn't Satan himself appear as an angel of light (II Cor. 11:14). Repentance is considered unnecessary because Unity teaches reincarnation and man himself is a God.

155

Unity and Salvation

Unity speaks of sin, redemption and atonement but does not give the words the same meaning as the Scriptures do. Unity denies the existence of a literal heaven or hell. Because Unity believes in reincarnation it also teaches that man's heaven or hell depends on himself. According to Charles Fillmore, a person will receive heaven or hell on this earth. Man is his own savior.

In Vol. 58 of *Unity Magazine,* July, 1922, No. 49, Charles Fillmore summed up the Unity teaching on salvation with these words: "Unity teaches that the eternal life taught and demonstrated by Jesus is not gained by dying, but by purifying the body until it becomes the undying habitation of the soul." Unity does not teach the eternal life offered according to the Word of God. Jesus said, "There are many rooms in my Father's house, and I am going to prepare a place for you. I would not tell you this if it were not so. And after I go and prepare a place for you, I will come back and take you to myself, so that you will be where I am" (John 14:2, 3).

Reincarnation

Unity teaches the Hindu doctrine of reincarnation. When one examines the Unity cult it is easy to see how ancient errors have been presented in an attractive, modern wrapping. The Unity statement of faith, Article 22, affirms:

> We believe that the dissolution of spirit, soul and body, caused by death, is annulled by rebirth of the same spirit and soul in another body here on earth. We believe the repeated incarnations of man to be a merciful provision of our loving Father to the end that all may have opportunity to attain immortality through regeneration, as did Jesus.

Unity emphasizes that man keeps coming back to earth learning to live better and better each time. This is no different from the teachings of the Hindus. They say that we are suffering for sins we committed in a previous life and each time we live we atone for them. The strange thing is that no one seems to remember what he did wrong in his past life. If we do not know for what sin we are atoning we will probably repeat the offense.

Summary

Charles W. Ferguson in his book, *The New Books of Revelation*, appraises Unity as follows:

Thus it is that, with much wind and high sales pressure, the Unity School of Christianity serves the multitudes. It gets results. It offers a philosophism that sounds well and works better. It has demonstrated its success for the millions of adherents who have been swept into the paper fold. Underpinning its vast machinery are of course, the cases in which it has cured diseases of every sort and its glib promise of physical immortality to its followers. The machinery is not to be despised.

We have in Unity an enormous mail order concern dispensing health and happiness on the large scale of modern business enterprise. It is mass production in religion, and its work is carried on shrewdly and systematically with infinite pains to capitalize upon the old demand and extend the market. It is the work of a retired realtor, and his inspired wife, and with its tedious array of tabulated facts and its insufferable efficiency, it suggests pretty well what Americans want in the realm of the spirit. (Doubleday-Doran and Company, Garden City, 1929, p. 250.)

C. *Reverend Moon*

You may again want to ask me, "With what authority do you say these things?" I spoke with Jesus Christ in the spirit world. And I spoke with John the Baptist. This is my authority.

Sun Myung Moon made the above statement in a speech October 28, 1983, in New Orleans, Louisiana. I have often wondered where Mr. Moon got his new revelations. Now, at last, we know; his revelations come from the dead!

Recently I was given a copy of Arthur Ford's book, *Unknown but Known*. Arthur Ford became well known through his widely televised seance with Bishop Pike many years ago. In this book, Mr. Ford indicates that he had several sittings with Sun Myung Moon, the first reported on November 2, 1964.

Arthur Ford's spirit guide, Fletcher, proclaimed that Mr. Moon was the voice of the creative mind and that he would be the front runner of the New Age Movement. He said, "Mr. Moon in deep meditation can project himself and be seen just as Jesus has been able to project himself and be seen by the saints. This is one of the marks of the messiahs always,'' (*Unknown but Known,* p. 112).

One of the most revealing aspects of the accounts of these seances is that the New Age Movement is referred to by the spirit guide, Fletcher. In discussing the mission of Mr. Moon, Fletcher said: "He is one of those who will be the human instrument through whom the World Teacher will be able to speak. And he was chosen because the New Age can be ushered in only through the eastern gate of the City of God." The spirits claimed that Sun Myung Moon was, as the Teacher, the Leader, the Chosen One, an instrument through whom God reveals his will. Speaking of Moon, Fletcher said:

> The Holy Spirit has not been quiet—and he has not been inactive. But there come periodically in the history of the race moments when the Holy Spirit has to individualize almost completely in some person— who becomes the instrument who will enable others to catch the Spirit and see the Spirit, and know the Spirit. And so they go in all directions, never separated from the source, but always individualized. . . .
> Sun Myung Moon is the one I have been talking about. I have been speaking for a group of people here. This group seems to surround him. And the power that flows through him, the intelligence, is not just one —it is a great group of people. And they seem all to draw their inspiration and their knowledge from One Source—and they seem to pour it symbolically into a pool and in some strange symbolical way that pool becomes Sun Myung Moon (*Unknown but Known,* p. 118).

According to Ford, Fletcher, the spirit guide, spoke as the representative of several deceased people. One of those mentioned was Kim Koo, represented as a martyred patriot in Korea. Koo, speaking through Fletcher, is quoted as saying:

> This man [Moon] has a message—this man has no message—but the Holy Spirit, the Spirit of Truth, can speak through Moon more clearly— more completely—than he is able to speak through any one individual today. It may take a long time for his truth to be realized in the hearts of men. But even the Christ had to have his John the Baptist to herald him—and then, after he came, he had to gather around him a group— and after his death that group bore witness—and it's a long time. (*Unknown but Known,* p. 123).

Mr. Moon in his book, *Christianity in Crisis* (p. 98), says of his teachings, "These are hidden truths presented to you as new revelations. You have heard me speak from the Bible. If you believe the Bible you must believe what I am saying." Mr. Moon asserts that his words are equal in authority to the Bible.

Many times I have wondered where Mr. Moon got his new revelations. Now I have found out Mr. Moon's secret. His revelations come from the dead.

12

GAMES PEOPLE PLAY

A. *Ouija Board*

The insistent ring of the telephone drew me out of my sleep. A quick look at the clock revealed it was 2:00 a.m. As I picked up the receiver a frantic voice on the other end said, "Brother Ben, I'm sorry to wake you at this hour but I need your help desperately." The caller was a minister in Canada and at that moment one of his church members was hysterical over the possibility of a death prophecy coming true. The woman had played with a ouija board as a child and the board had given the message that she would die on her 30th birthday. The woman had lived with that fear for many years and now her 30th birthday had arrived. She was hysterical. After a lengthy conversation we were able to convince her that the prophecy would only come true if she fulfilled it herself—as Satan wished!

This situation is not unusual. The ouija board is not a toy but a highly sophisticated tool of Satan designed to destroy the souls of men, women and children.

What Is a Ouija Board?

The board is made out of masonite or wood in a rectangular shape about 18" x 12". On the board are the numbers 0-9 and the letters of the alphabet. The words *yes and no* are at opposite upper corners and the word *goodbye* is at the bottom. Along with the board comes a heart-shaped tripod. To operate the board, one or more people place their hands on the tripod (pointer). Questions are asked by the participants and the pointer slides over the board spelling out the messages.

Ouija Board - A Tool of Divination

The suggestion is usually made that the users of the ouija board subconsciously or consciously push the pointer to make it spell out messages. This may be true in some cases. However many people tell of information received from the board which could only come from a super-natural source. There is no power in the board itself, however there is power in the person who plays it.

The word *divination* means the art of obtaining information from the spirit world and this is forbidden by God (Deut. 18:10; Acts 16:16). In order to understand divination we must remember that we are made in the image of God. God is a spirit and we are spirits in a human body. We are aware of our five senses: taste, touch, sight, hearing, and smell. However there is also a sixth sense and this has to do with our spirit. There is a battle going on for this spirit as shown in Ephesians 6:12. We yield either to God or to Satan. When a person puts his hands on the ouija board pointer, he yields his spirit to foreign intelligences which the Bible calls demons, and the result is divination.

A classic example of divination is given in Acts 16:16. Paul was being followed by a slave girl who had a spirit of divination. A look at this passage reveals: (1) it is possible to be controlled by a spirit (see also Mark 5), (2) demons can tell the truth. These characteristics also apply to the ouija board.

Satan's Inconsistency Makes Him Dangerous

People say to me, "I have played with the ouija board and it has never worked for me. Why?" Satan is cunning and it is this very cunning which makes him so dangerous. Church leaders who don't believe the ouija board works will not teach against it, and in fact will treat it as a harmless toy. It is not a toy—it is a satanic tool!

Personal Experiences

When I first started using the ouija board I noticed that I could feel a personality taking me over and then the spirit would identify itself. It would spell out its name or give a type of identification (I recall one that would make three circles, a cross and then spell its name) and then go on with the message. Sometimes the pointer moved so fast that someone would have to call out the letters while another wrote them down.

People have told me they received messages which made no sense at all until they were read backwards. Of course this is fascinating but it is an unholy fascination.

I encountered one spirit which never identified itself, and instead of going very fast it went very slowly. Before it started spelling the message out, all of us would sense an eerie presence in the room. Then the message would come over and over again, "All is dark, pray for us." At the time the teaching of spiritualism led me to believe this was a wandering soul who had died, didn't realize it and was seeking a body to use.

Who Uses the Ouija Board?

Children are not the only ones who get involved in the ouija board. I am aware of elderly people, especially women who have lost their husbands, and have taken up the ouija board in an attempt to continue communicating with their loved one. Use of the board runs the gamut of all ages from the very young to the elderly.

Often children are introduced to the board at slumber parties. The lights are turned out and a candle lit for effect. The children know that in order for the board to work they have to call upon a spirit so they decide on a deceased aunt who was always telling when people were going to die or when babies would be born. They call upon this dead aunt and ask her to give them messages generally dealing with who and when they will marry. There is much hilarity but then something happens. The name of one of the girls is spelled out and then a message follows which tells the date the girl will die. Satan knows exactly which child to pick—one who will easily be overcome with fear. Occasionally these messages come true but it is through self-fulfillment. Satan is a murderer; he is a destroyer (John 8:44).

Bud Clapp, a professor at Ozark Bible College, tells of an experience he had with a death prophecy. A young man came to Bud's house to see him, however, Bud was out of town. When Bud's wife explained that he would not be back until the following Tuesday, the young man said "It would be too late." He had received a message that he would die before Monday. Bud saw him in the morgue on Monday. The young man shot himself over the weekend.

Several years ago I had occasion to speak on a Christian radio station in Spokane, Washington. The moderator was a young Christian lady. She told me that her mother played with the ouija board all night long. She related that one night she told her mother it was foolish and accused her of pushing the pointer around with her fingers. Her mother then held her hand about 4" above the pointer. Her hand and the pointer then began moving across the board at the same time. Her mother's hand, obviously being directed by something other than her mother, was supplying energy to the pointer without touching it. The moderator said she was shocked and told her mother it was of the devil.

Consequences

Use of the ouija board does four things:

1. It is in conflict with Jesus' teaching in Matthew 6 that we should not worry about tomorrow.
2. It is a violation of God's law concerning divination.
3. It encourages demonic activity.
4. It can lead to dependency on the board and an unbalancing of the mind.

Christians must realize that occultism is dangerous. Involvement in occult practices binds persons psychologically and spiritually. Occult practices are opposed to Christianity. The church should clearly condemn occultism, as does the Bible.

B. *Dungeons and Dragons*

Satan is flexible. He will appeal to man on whatever basis works. To the occultist he says, "I'll prove the reality of the spirit world." To the humanists, he says, "There is no such thing as a spirit world or demons. It's all a fantasy game, so do your own thing and have fun."

Dungeons and Dragons in Spiritualism

My personal knowledge of Spiritualism makes it very easy for me to recognize the influence Satan has upon those who play D & D.

1. The chief controller plays God.
2. The names of many of the characters given to the players are the same names given in the Bible to Satan's Kingdom.

    Moloch - the fire god to whom children were offered to be burned alive (Deut. 12:31; Lev. 20:1-6).
    Baal - idol to whom human sacrifices were offered.
    Incubus - a demon involving supernatural sexual immorality.
    Belial, Ashtareth, Diana - the worship of many of these gods involved homosexuality.

3. The players become undisciplined in their minds and overindulge in fantasies and act out murder, violence, and sexual fantasies. Proverbs 23:7 says "As a man thinks so he is." Jesus tells us a man can commit adultery in his heart. To act out these characters in a so-called harmless game is tantamount to satanic worship.

Satan—a Roaring Lion

According to *Eternity* magazine, 46% of all D & D enthusiasts are children ages 10-14, 20% are ages 15-17. The popularity of D & D reflects the void among a great segment of our society. This void is being filled by magic, fantasy and make-believe in such movies as "Star Wars" (with world box office receipts of $480 million), "Dragon Slayer," "Rosemary's Baby," "The Omen," "The Anti-Christ," and other horror films.

Victor Ernest, a former spiritualist and now a Christian, in a similar article to this one says his personal background and knowledge of the kingdom of Satan make it very easy for him to recognize the devil in D & D.

To date over three million Americans are playing this game in schools, colleges and homes, many of them Christian. Parents, be on guard. Satan goes around like a roaring lion, seeking souls to kill and destroy (I Peter 5:8). Don't let him destroy your child.

C. *Halloween*

Many Christian parents are concerned about what Halloween really is. We know that it is of Druidical origin which means that it was part of the Druid religion. Druidism revolved around the worship of evil spirits, and offerings to them to insure the welfare of the worshipers.

The Origin of Halloween

The name of the festival in early days (and it is still found in Ireland) meant "Satan's Watch." It was the night given over to Satan and his demons to work all the evil they wanted in the hope they would leave people unmolested the rest of the year.

Spiritualism, witchcraft, is very real and we should not be providing our children with this opportunity for involvement. Many, if not all of our Halloween customs have their roots in these ancient beliefs. The witch, of course, is the personification of evil which is a substitute for Satan. The jack-o-lantern symbolizes the fire that was kept burning in the houses of those who feared Satan's worst.

What Halloween Really Means

Dressing up in costumes and "trick or treating" to the neighbors is a carry over of the idea of making an offering to Satan and to the spirits to appease them. "Trick or treating" is a modern form of saying "offering or revenge." The grotesque and horrible masks our young people wear making themselves look like skeletons, dead people, or horrible monsters are symbolizing Satan inspiring fear to get an offering.

Satan likes Halloween celebrations because this is a glorification of evil. Most people naturally do not think of it in this way. We believe it is all done in fun. But when we poke fun and joke about the spirit world, we are encouraging ourselves and our children to believe that this doesn't really exist. When we allow our children to dress up like witches and ghosts we are allowing them to treat lightly what God treats seriously in His Word. Those who don't know about the origin and meaning of Halloween are feeding their own belief into the Word of God when they treat lightly and celebrate what God hates. Satan camouflages himself amidst fun and gaiety and gets people to belittle his power and activity among men or even completely deny it. It is a very clever trick of the enemy.

An Alternative for Today

Satan is getting bolder in the United States. Occult practices are springing up all over America. Halloween parties provide a perfect setting for these. Often at these parties there is fortune telling, ouija boards, seances, and things of that nature. We can't afford to have our children participate in these activities.

We realize the problems this creates because it will be said, "everybody" is dressing up to go "trick or treating." October 31 is not evil of itself. It is what we do with it that matters. Let's work at substituting good fun for bad. We can start working through our church. Instead of having a Halloween party, have a fun night—games, refreshments, and perhaps even a film. The children can dress up— maybe a clown night, an old-fashioned night, or even Bible character night. Have a party! Have fun! Let it be harmless fun and let us glorify our Lord Jesus Christ—not His adversary.

Don't TRICK your child but TREAT your child!

13

THE SEDUCTION OF SOCIETY

A. *Pornography*

The church has been called by Christ to be the salt and light. By default our silence has allowed America to deteriorate to such an extent that it makes Sodom and Gomorrah look like a Sunday school picnic. We are handing our children a culture that is morally ravaged beyond anything we received from our parents.

During the last several months since I became actively involved in fighting pornography, I have been sickened by the lust laden character of this evil. I absolutely refuse to keep silent and will fight this insidious evil which is destroying our families till the day I die.

In this article I wish to share with you:

(1) The porno epidemic.

(2) Why? the crisis.

(3) The effect of pornography on the lives of millions of Americans.

(4) How to fight pornography and win.

In his book *The Seduction of Society* William A. Stanmeyer said, "The spread of pornography is slowly poisoning American society. Once obscenity was largely confined to "adult book stores" in sleazy neighborhoods of major cities. Now it is found in suburban shopping malls, on prime time television, and in glossy general interest magazines. The victims of this "victimless crime" number in the millions. They include women and children who are exploited by pornography, those who are raped and killed in obscenity-related crimes and millions of males whose sexuality is warped by degrading pornographic images.

And yet, how much do we worry about pornography? Too many Americans regard it indifferently, as other people's private vices, or as the price we pay for free speech. But the Constitution does not protect obscenity, and "private" vices have swiftly become a public menace.

There is a growing danger of continued indifference to pornography. It threatens our families, warps our minds, and contaminates our culture. It is time we learn how to eliminate this "quiet, but devastating social crisis."

The Frog Is Cooked

Why has pornography been allowed to be so prevalent in our society today? Perhaps the answer can be found in this story. How do you boil a frog? Well, you certainly cannot plop him into a pot of boiling water — he will just hop out as fast as he can. Instead, place the frog in a pot of tepid water, and place the pot over a slow cooking flame. As the temperature slowly rises, the frog, being cold blooded, easily adapts to his metabolism little by little to the heat. Soon the placidly content frog will be sitting happily in a pot of boiling water, unaware of his danger because he adapted slowly to his environment.

The analogy is clear. This flood of filth did not pour out into the towns and cities of our nation suddenly. It came upon us slowly, bit by bit, working away at the foundation of our morality.

The deception has been gradual like a slow growing cancer and now the infection is oozing out on the screen in films, video tapes, and sexual innuendoes on television. Pornography is a way of life in the entertainment industry.

During the 1940's to 1950's the moral tone of society was

reasonably high, but gradually the cancer of pornography began to infiltrate society. Something happened around about the 1960's. I believe it was a combination of Hugh Hefner and his "playboy philosophy," the explosive situation of the Berkley and Columbia student riots, the general rejection of customary beliefs in morality and religion, the scandal of the "flower children," and collegiate promiscuity.

Moral attitudes have changed, not all at once but gradually, and now the public is conditioned to an acceptance of obscenity unknown in the history of mankind since Sodom and Gomorrah.

The Subtlety of Soft-Porn

The truly dangerous pornography is not the hard-core porn. Most people can obviously see it's rotten to the core. The real danger is the soft-core "playboy philosophy."

Playboy porn is far more than just dirty pictures. It is the foundation for a world view that educates, titilates and stimulates men and women into hedonistic living.

Playboy is the most effective magazine in achieving the goals of the sexual revolution. The average non-Christian says, "I don't mind *Playboy*; it's the really gross stuff that should be banned."

Fortune magazine in the August 12, 1981, issue commented that *Playboy* is "the only girlie magazine acceptable for family reading and display on coffee tables."

This type of pornography has been cleverly coupled with articles written by intellectual humanists.

The philosophy of the articles in *Playboy* is much more subversive than the pictures themselves. However, the pictures are needed in order to influence the reader to brainwash him into a certain life-style.

For example a man may not reject his wife strictly on the written word, however, when you couple the written word with photos of beautiful nude women in provocative poses you fuel the fires with erotic thoughts. He then looks at his wife and becomes dissatisified.

He is also encouraged in the many articles written to get involved in wife swapping. I shudder to think how many marriages *Playboy* and similar magazines have destroyed.

Playboy — Manual for the High Achiever

The *Playboy* magazine equips its readers to enjoy the very best in lifestyle — clothes, expensive cars, stereo equipment, restaurants, and vacations.

The impression is given that their readers are a brand of liberated males. The playboy learns that marriage can be expensive and that women can be obtained on a cost-basis factor. Why go through all the hardship of work to keep a woman and children, whn you can obtain sex for just the price of a dinner and a few drinks. Plus, you have the added advantage of spending all your hard-earned money on yourself. Yes, sir — you can have your cake and eat it too. You can have the benefit of marriage without its responsibilities. This philosophy has had such an effect on individual males that its readership numbers into the millions.

Fantasy

In order to have a lifestyle laid down by the *Playboy* manual, the rich living is obviously only possible for the favored few. Therefore, they must offer the reader an internal thought life that is even more superior to the external reality. So, an intense brainwashing is performed on the reader's mind. The *Playboy* offers new experiences and variety. This type of thinking leads a person into a subjective experiential lifestyle of sex.

In the book *The High Cost of Indifference* March Bell explains how FANTASY: BECOMES A DEADLY REALITY. He says, "Popular pornographic magazines, especially *Playboy* and *Penthouse* for men and *Cosmopolitan* for women constantly offer exciting testimonies of varied new sexual experiences usually to be adopted or at least considered by the readership." *Penthouse* accomplishes this through its FORUM section (also a separate publication). Each month numerous sexual conquests are erotically recounted to ensure the reader that men and women everywhere are trying new partners, places, techniques, and so on, to enhance sexual experiences. In related articles, a scientific support team of medical advisors with university credentials reassures the reader that healthy sexual experiences can be enhanced by wife swapping, bisexuality, cross dressing, and the life.

Cosmopolitan, although tamer, provides the same experiential enthusiasm for women. Articles such as "Can Adultery Save Your Marriage?" and "Is He The Right Lover?" appear in every issue.

The social costs of experiential faith have been tremendous, especially in the area of divorce. Once the playboy commits himself to new experiences, the cost benefit analogies of monogamous sexuality begin to slowly undermine marriage. The playboy asks himself, "Why put up with all that marriage requires when new sexual encounters are so easily attained?" The magazines promise that until the man actually breaks away, pornography will see him through.

Playboy offers the readers a different way to spend his money. It is simply a lot cheaper to obtain sex than to hve the worry and concern of a family. The goal in pornographic sex is nothing more than an achievement of an orgasm. It is so much less costly than marriage.

Jesus said, "You have heard that it was said, 'Do not commit adultery.' But I tell you that anyone who looks at a woman lustfully has already committed adultery with her in his heart" (Matt. 5:27-28). I shudder to think of the 20 million men reading *Playboy*.

Sex Without Persons

In the book *The High Cost of Indifference* Marc Bell wrote, "Perhaps the most tragic harm caused by pornography is its destruction of sex itself." Pornography multiplies real or imagained sex partners to such an extent that mutuality to a one wife relationship becomes boring and unsatisfactory.

The most graphic example of sex without persons is found in the adult bookstore where pornographic films are shown in a private booth 25 cents for 2 minutes segments.

They who cannot achieve the dream world of the *Playboy* mansion lifestyle finally end up in the adult bookstore. This eventually leads to the raunchy hard porn and then the biggest tragedy of all — they look for the easiest people to exploit — THE CHILDREN.

Children the Victims

America has more than one million runaway children a year. Many of them run from home to escape incest. Perverse parents sexually abuse their children. Adult bookstores sell a child seducer's manual titled: *Lust For Fun* which shows in detail how to entice a little girl from a school yard or playground, take her home, undress her, have sex, and then be able to hide all traces that you, or anyone had ever abused her. Pornographers do not know when to stop. Be assured that they never will unless angry parents, responsible citizens, and concerned Christians rise up and say, "We have had enough!" NO MORE. ENOUGH IS ENOUGH. It is time to declare war on those who pander pornography. We have a responsibility; we are called by God to expose the evil deeds of darkness (Eph. 5:11-12).

What Can You Do?

(1) Read the *New Testament* to discover what "Agape" love is. Ask God to give you that love. You will read and see that love in the life of Christ and the life of early Christians.

(2) Then out of love to your fellow man proceed with the following: Complain about pornography, keep on complaining, it works. Complain to City Attorneys, District Attorneys, Mayors, City Councilmen, Congressmen, Governors, newspaper editors, retailers, distributors, television station managers, and theater owners.

(3) Collect samples of pornographic magazines. Get receipts, or have someone with you as an eye-witness to the sale. Show the magazines to church groups, PTA groups, Civic groups — groups which, most likely, do not know the trash being sold and — upon being shown — vigorously, steadily, fight to remove it. Also take samples to local police officials, district attorney's office or city attorney's office to swear in formal complaints.

(4) Every time you enter a store, check the magazine and bookracks. If you find any pornography, take it off the shelf and show it to the manager. In many cases, store manager's don't realize what magazine and book jobbers leave on their shelves.

(5) Boycott. If a store refuses to stop selling pornography (including *Playboy*) don't trade with him and circulate petitions to get other people not to trade. Send petitions to store owners. Meanwhile, actively trade with stores who refuse to sell pornography and circulate petitions telling them you appreciate them.

Join CDL, Citizens for Decency through Law, address 2331 West Royal Palm Road, Suite 105, Phoenix, Arizona 85021.

My heartfelt thanks to Neil Gallagher, March Bell and Paul Tanner for making much of the above material available.

B. *Humanism in Our Schools*

On March 4, 1987, a federal judge in Mobile, Alabama, ruled that 44 textbooks were to be banned from use in the state's schools. He held the books to be in violation of the First Amendment because they illegally promoted a godless humanist religion. Parents who had raised this issue were labeled "book burners" and "censors." These parents had become alarmed by several things that were gradually becoming apparent to them. Questioning of family-held values and beliefs was becoming very prominent, even amongst younger children. Academic skills were on the decline. Understanding of American history and of the United States role in the world was found to be far different from what previous generations of Americans had grown up with.

A Trust Betrayed

Having once had blind faith in the educational system to which they had entrusted their children's minds and futures, as, indeed, do most Americans, these parents now began to ask the question, "Exactly what are our children learning at school?" An investigation into the textbooks being used in their children's education provided some very disconcerting answers. One history book which devoted 35 pages to telling the story of the Pilgrims, never once mentioned God or the faith in Him that led these people to the new world. A "health class" text discussed the options available to a pregnant teenager, among which was a toll-free number that gave abortion counseling. Other questionable passages were rampant, and incensed over the distorted view their children were being subjected to, these parents banded together to do something about it.

Religion in the Schools

Defense attorneys subsequently appealed this decision on the grounds that religion must be kept out of the schools. Publishers could not mention God in their texts, they argued, and likewise, morals, with their intrinsic religious bias, could not be presented. In the name of "separation of church and state" educators are systematically eradicating all reference to God and to the existence of a thriving and widespread faith in God from the American schoolchild's educational experience. The attorneys cried, "Censorship" at the attempt to ban these books. But they voice no concern over the censorship that took place in the very writing of the texts. They cry, "No religion in the schools" and they knowingly, or unknowingly, promote the cause of another religion in its place.

In 1961 the Supreme Court stated that "among religions in this country which do not teach what would generally be considered a belief in the existence of God are Buddhism, Taoism,, Ethical Culture, Secular Humanism, and others." Humanism is a recognized, established religion. Under the protection of the First Amendment, Humanists have pursued one of their primary goals — the incorporation of their religion into the midstream of American life. And as 19th century Humanist Wilhelm von Humboldt wrote, "Whatever we wish to see introduced into a life or a nation must first be introduced into its schools."

The Battlefield Defined

This quote from *The Humanist* magazine, dated January/February, 1983, entitled, "A Religion For A New Age," declares the strategy that the Humanists have chosen, "I am convinced that the battle for humankind's future must be waged and won in the public school classroom by teachers who correctly perceive their role as the proselytizers of a new faith. These teachers must embody the same selfless dedication as the most rabid fundamentalist preachers, for they will be ministers of another sort, utilizing a classroom instead of a pulpit to convey humanist values in whatever subjects they teach, regardless of the educational level — preschool, daycare or large state university.

"The classroom must and will become an arena of conflict between the old and the new — the rotting corpse of Christianity, together with all its adjacent evils and misery and the new faith of

Humanism, resplendent in its promise of a world in which the never-realized Christian ideal of 'love thy neighbor' will finally be achieved."

The Strategy

In light of the above statement, consider these excerpts from textbooks in general use across our country:

"For a very few, religion can still provide a special sense of . . . selfhood, but cannot adequately define the entire person." (*Introduction to the Behavioral Sciences; An Inquiry Approach*, Holt, Rinehart and Winston, 1969.)

"A great many myths deal with the idea of rebirth. Jesus, Dionysus, Odin, and many other traditional figures are represented as having died, after which they were reborn, or arose from the dead." (*Psychology For You*, Oxford Book Co., 1973.)

These examples are taken from texts geared for upper grades. Presenting religion to teenagers in this poor light is bad enough, but now consider the content of this English book for *third graders*:

"One way to make up a myth is to think of a question like 'Why do men have pain?' Now, imagine a time when men did not have pain. Pretend that the first men on earth went around without ever feeling pain. Next imagine that some kind of god walked among men and something happened. Maybe a man did something bad or made a bad mistake. Because of this, the god punished men, giving them pain for the rest of their days." (*Communicating*, The Health English Series, Grade 3, Heath and Co., 1973.)

What place has such a subtle and manipulative undermining of a child's religious beliefs in the context of an English lesson? The answer comes from the Humanist camp, "And how does a God die? Quite simply because all His religionists have been converted to another religion and there is no one left to make the *children* believe they need Him. We need only insure that our schools teach only secular knowledge. If we could achieve this, God would be dead and shortly due for a funeral service." (G. Richard Bozarth, *The American Atheist*.)

A most significant and particularly frightening change has taken place in history books. The role of the Bible and Christianity in the founding of this nation is consistently censored or distorted. Not one religious quote comes from such prominent believers who shaped our nation's history as John Adams, Benjamin Franklin, or William Penn. Likewise, examples of great patriotism or adherence to American ideals have been eliminated. Patrick Henry is briefly referred to as a statesman of the times, and nowhere can be found the historic words, "Give me liberty or give me death!"

One history teacher tells the following story, "I even got into trouble last year for just teaching right out of a secular history book. It mentioned B.C. and A.D. and I had to 'put fires out' because I brought out the dateline and told how history points the years before and after the coming of Christ. The fact that I would mention that brought the wrath down upon me. This bothers me because it appears that there is a structure there of some kind that is really fighting hard to develop an agnostic or atheistic culture." (From Phyllis Schlafly's, *Child Abuse in the Classroom*.)

Who's Behind It

It seems that a general awareness of this "structure" is gradually dawning upon the parents and teachers of American schoolchildren. Further evidence of such an influence being deliberately and purposefully at work in our public education system comes once again from the Humanistic themselves. Author Tim LaHaye in his book, *The Race For the 21st Century*, gives this account, "At an education seminar for about a thousand teachers, Dr. Chester Pierce, a Harvard University professor of education and psychiatry announced: 'Every child in America entering school at the age of five is mentally ill because he comes to school with certain allegiances toward our founding fathers, toward ur elected officials, toward his parents, toward a belief in a supernatural being, toward the sovereignty of this nation as a separate entity. It's up to you teachers to make all of these sick children well by creating the international children of the future.'"

This quote is from the journal of the National Education Association, *Today's Education*, dated January, 1969: "For one thing, the basic role of the teacher will change noticeably. Ten years hence, it will be more accurate to term him a learning clinician. This title is intended to convey the idea that schools are becoming clinics, whose purpose is to provide individualized psychosocial treatment for the student.''

In that same year, the president of the National Education Association (NEA) bluntly stated that ''within ten years I think this organization will control the qualifications for entrance into this (teaching) profession and for the privilege of remaining in the profession.'' The NEA, an organization firmly entrenched with the Humanist movement, wields a great deal of influence over what gets into our public schools' curriculum and who gets to teach it. Its stated purposes and goals are an outright threat to American an Judeo-Christian principles. How close has it come to realizing its objectives?

A Foot In The Door

Let's look at two major programs that the NEA has already succeeded in incorporating into the basic education of our children. (These programs have been funded by federal tax dollars.)

Values Clarification — also known as situation ethics, moral reasoning, higher critical thinking, and other similar jargon. These techniques are actual methods of therapy. In practice, this ''therapy'' education is a system of changing a child's values through the use of attitude questionnaires, psychological games, and forcing the child to make adult decisions about such topics as suicide, murder, marriage, divorce, abortion, and adoption. Children are repeatedly asked to analyze their values and beliefs. They are told that there are no ''right'' or ''wrong'' answers, but at the same time are psychologically pressured to adjust their values or beliefs to conform to those of the majority. Comments made by an NEA spokesman at an NEA conference declare that ''The school cannot allow parents to influence the kinds of values education their children receive at school. We must challenge values.''

Sex Education — Students are taught to select and clarify their own values. Teachers mustn't moralize — except against the belief that one set of sexual values may be right. As one teacher put it, ''As sex educators, we are not telling them what to do, we are teaching them what we know — as facts, not as truth.'' The NEA works hand in hand with Planned Parenthood and supports its goal to ''modify attitudes and to abolish the arbitrary and out-moded restrictions which continue to limit the individual's freedom of choice in fertility matters."

The Remedy

Textbooks have become a strategic weapon in the hands of the enemies of Jesus Christ and His people, a carefully designed tool for winning away the minds and souls of His very children. Brothers and Sisters, we cannot sit back and let this go on unchecked. It will take great effort, but the tide can be stemmed. Two books I have used as resource material are, *Child Abuse In The Classroom*, by Phyllis Schlafly, published by Crossway Books, and *What Are They Teaching Our Children?*, by Mel and Norma Gabler, published by Victor Books. Both give detailed descriptions of offensive teaching practices and textbooks, and also give excellent practical advice for taking up the fight. The Gablers, in particular, have spent twenty-five years in this battle and are experts in the field. They have even included their address and phone number to make themselves available to others who are moved to act in this arena. Almost single-handedly the Gablers have brought textbook publishers to account before committees that have rejected books and demanded changes to be made. But their crusade cannot be carried on alone. It's time for great numbers of parents and Christians to take up the slack.

Parents, start looking at what's in those textbooks your children bring home, and go to their classrooms to examine those they don't. Not surprisingly, many schools now have a policy of not allowing books to be taken out of the school. If you find objectionable material, show it to other parents as well. The books I've mentioned can give you further information as to how to present your objections to the school, but the important thing is to make yourself aware of what is going on and then to act. Question your children as to discussions and activities that go on during classtime. Follow up on anything that sounds suspicious. Expect to take a lot of flak for getting involved, but don't forget what's at stake. Take comfort in our Lord Jesus' words, "All men will hate you because of me, but he who stands firm to the end will be saved." Let us not abandon the little children of America to the godlessness and futility of secular Humanism.

C. *Heavy Metal Rock and Your Child*

Like everything else Satan will take something good and make it evil. Over the past three decades Satan has taken good music and gradually brainwashed our children into listening to so-called Rock Stars screaming and howling their message of sex, suicide, satanism, despair and death.

The Rock and Roll groups of the 1980's have reached a new low. Parents are going to have to take strong action to destroy this satanic music before it destroys their children.

History of Rock and Roll

Historically rock music had a beginning in 1954 in Cleveland, Ohio, when disc jockey Alan Freed was searching for a term to describe the response of teenagers who were caught up in the musical revolution that was just beginning. Not only was it a musical revolution, but as millions of female eyes became glued to the pelvis of Elvis, it also became a sexual revolution. The term rock 'n roll is a descriptive expression from the ghetto community which refers to fornication taking place in the back seat of cars in drive-in movies. (*Our Music and Morals* by Batsell Barnett Bacher, and *Upread* — a magazine for better living, January/February, 1981.)

Christians must remove their blinders and recognize the significance of these satanic vultures masquerading as religious ceremonies which we have come to accept under the title of "Rock Concerts," "M.T.V.," heavy metal and discos.

The Source

Satan is reproducing himself by recruiting growing numbers of children and youth raised in families of our Judeo-Christian republic to satanic cultures. They are being recruited to organized satanic cults.

In order to understand the strategy of Satan we must be on the alert to his ephemerals. These are groups that last a short time and then migrate from membership in one cult to another — from Hara Krishna to Transcendental Meditation to the Moonies to The Way International, etc., etc. Eventually these peoples' minds become so distorted, they become psychotic and cannot tell the difference between fantasy and reality.

Rock and Mysticism

In 1981 a process was set in motion by the aging Rolling Stones band. This was the beginning of a new era — "Satan Rock." Other groups quickly caught on: KISS (Knights in Satan's Service), AC/DC, Ozzie Osborne, Black Sabbath and David Lee Roth. The leaders of of the bands set themselves up as priests of the devil and their "rock concerts" were to become satanic ceremonies.

The reason for the promotion of Satanic Rock was because of disturbing trends in the music industry. In August, 1981, the Gallup Youth Poll discovered that the 13-18 year old attendance at rock concerts had dropped by 12% while youth attendance at symphony concerts rose 3%.

Atlantic Records of Los Angeles decided to do something about their falling sales and brought the Rolling Stones led by Mick Jagger out of retirement with the help of media hype — *Newsweek* and *Time* magazines. They promoted Mick Jagger and his band as a living legend and 90,000 youth attended the J.F.K. Memorial Stadium in Philadelphia.

The group, Black Sabbath, goes out of its way to promote Satanism. Their songs are filled with demonic references. Titles are: "Wizard," "Voodoo," and "Stonehenge." Group member, Bill Ward, believes Satan is God. Another member, Greezer Butler, claims he is Lucifer. Their main composer, Tony Tommi, admits his main interest in life is witchcraft.

The trend to mysticism first was made prominent by the Beatles. George Harrison's albums, "Somewhere in England" and "They Call You Christ," "Yishnu," "Buddha, Jehovah Our Lord," are permeated with mysticism. Obviously he believes all religions are alike.

The celebrated "Beach Boys," chosen to represent an all American image for July 4th celebration at the White House, promoted Transcendental Meditation. Beach Boy, Mike Love has been a T.M.'er for years. They dedicated an album, M.I.U., to the Maharishi International University in Fairfield, Iowa. The school was founded by the Maharishi Mahish Yogi.

The message on the album was filled with persuasive messages to get involved in T.M. and no doubt influenced many of our youth.

This writer went to Fairfield, Iowa and warned the city council of the foolhardiness of selling the college to this occult organization. Now they are sorry.

The occult today has become the "in thing" for famous movie stars — Shirley MacLaine (her belief in reincarnation) is influencing millions. Her book, *Out On A Limb*, is a best seller. She is now making a film about this book. Guess who her advisors are? She contacts them at a seance.

Elizabeth Taylor brags about her Guru. She claims he saved her life.

Co-authors of the book (*Why Knock Rock*) page 76, write, "The late Jim Hendrix once told *Life* magazine, 'Atmospheres are going to come through, because music is a spiritual thing of it's own. You can hypnotize people with music and when you get people at the weakest point, you can preach to them into the subconscious what we want to say.' "

Ask yourself this: if the Holy Spirit can bless spiritual hymns and songs, and allow them to lift the soul of the listener, can the devil — the deceitful one, the counterfeiter, as he is called in Scripture — create the opposite effect? The answer is yes. And whether you consciously listen to the lyrics or not, your subconscious mind — which is the seat of the soul is influenced. Are you allowing avowed occultists to "preach" into your subconscious, as Hendrix boasted?

Rock and Violence

One of the most vulgar groups known for promoting violence are the Rolling Stones. According to the book, *Why Knock Rock*, it says, "Their hard and angry image, enhanced by media coverage of their urinating in public, grew to legendary proportions. In December, 1969, in Australia another concert forced the Stones to be thrown again into the limelight of infamy. It was at the festival at Altamout where the Hell's Angels had been hired to keep the peace. As Mick Jagger went through his diabolical routine prancing around for 'Jumping Jack Flash' and 'Sympathy For The Devil' the violence that had surfaced frequently throughout the festival broke loose. As Jagger watched, first in stunned silence and then while singing fearfully, a man was clubbed to death with pool cues, fists and chains, and stabbed five times — all within reach of the stage.''

At a Berlin concert, where crowds ran wild, setting fire to the stadium and vandalizing the shops outside, Jagger smoothly commented afterward, ''I entice the audience, of course I do.'' Despite the openness with which they express their intentions, the Stones have been allowed to roll on, quite successfully, producing 20 years worth of music sotted with drugs, sexual debauchery, violence and satanism.

It is obvious that teenagers identify with their rock stars. A Twisted Sister video entitled, ''We're Not Going To Take It,'' shows a boy throwing his father out of a window. Police believed this video inspired a boy to murder his father in New Mexico in the same fashion.

Thomas Radecki, chairman for the National Coalition on Television Violence (NCTV), estimated that 45 percent of some 1,200 rock videos monitored were of a violent nature. Dr. Radecki reported these types of videos desensitize individuals who watch this type of video.

Rock, Sex, and Pornography

Uppermost in the minds of the writers of rock music is sex. At one time the lyrics were obscure but this situation no longer exists. Many of the lyrics they sing are pure gutter language. The rock stars' lifestyles are no different.

Here are some comments of the rock stars themselves:

Andrew Oldham, manager of the Rolling Stones, said, ''Rock music is sex and you have to hit them (teenagers) in the face with it.''

Elton John advocated lesbianism. His song, ''All Girls Love Alice,'' is filled with suggestions to girls to practice lesbianism. The song ends with Alice committing suicide after she has had sexual relations with a number of married women.

Another song Elton John wrote, ''I Guess That's Why They Call It The Blues,'' deals with a heterosexual love affair. He also advocated prostitutuion in his song, ''Sweet Painted Lady.''

Led Zeppelin's recordings are simply filled with bizzare sexual behaviour. It is extremely difficult for me to put down the titles of his songs without offending the reader.

Dr. Hook and the Medicine Show is a seven man band who set pornography to music. In their album, "Sloppy Seconds" (referring to gang rape) they sing songs such as "Freakers Ball," which describes a pervert convention. Verse two suggests bringing drugs; verse three gives a list of guests that includes male and female homosexuals, sadists with leather fetishes, sado masochists and junkies.

Another sick artist is Alice Cooper. In his album, "Million Dollar Babies," he sings "I Love the Dead." This refers to necrophilia (sexual intercourse with a dead person). A verse goes as follows, "I love the dead before they're cold/the blueing flesh for me to hold."

The list of these filthy perverted musicians is endless. It seems the entertainment world has gone insane and our children are being dragged into the gutter by Satan's Pied Piper — the rock stars. Satan is alive and well as he prowls this planet devouring our children. History seems to be on a collision course and one wonders if there is any future for our children. Parents, I urge you to do everything in your power to stop this gutter music.

Rock and Suicide

Satan is a murderer (John 8:44). His disciples who carry out his wishes are the rock stars. One only has to look into the themes of the albums of the rock stars and it is not difficult to see who promotes suicide among our children.

There is no doubt that rock music influences have been the deciding factor in the lives of our unhappy children.

In Plano, Texas, Bruce saw the film "Pink Floyd and the Wall." It is about a rock singer who builds a wall around himself to shut out the unfriendly world. The teenager and his friend, Bill, began wearing rebel style leather jackets and boots. One night in a drag race, his friend Bill, who was the signal man, was accidently sideswiped by one of the cars and was killed.

Bruce kept to himself and told friends he would see Bill again "some sunny day," a line from Pink Floyd's songs. Bruce committed suicide in his car. The engine was running and in the car's cassette was the tape from the flim Pink Floyd — "Good-bye Cruel World."

Space does not permit the amount of suicides caused by rock and roll lyrics that encourage our children to "end it all."

185

The list of rock stars who have died via the drug route and suicides is endless and parents must take action.

If a teenager listens to his favorite rock star sing to him six hours a day telling him his solution is suicide, how can parents who average two minutes of conversation with their child each day convince him life is worth living.

In *Psychology Today*, Dr. V. Branfenbeuner points out that coming home to an empty house is probably one of the key problem areas . . . a lone child listening to rock music encouraging suicide can be fatal.

Lack of parental supervision is dangerous. We must spend more time with our children.

Standing on the Solid Rock

It is important that parents be informed on the subject of rock and roll. Visit the record department and as you scan the album covers, you may be shocked. You will probably think you're in an adult book store.

Listen to your local rock station. But be prepared for shocks, the music will be filled with pornography.

Buy the book, *Why Knock Rock*. It is important to be educated. On page 231 of this book the writer says, "Before you give your child your views on life, you must first give him yourself. You'll never seem smarter to him than during the times you just sit and listen. He needs to see you when you are available when he needs you."

Teacher and writer, Irene Primeau, says, "It has been said that values are caught not taught, and it is in the home that children catch the spiritual vision and emotional strength they need to cope with adverse and social pressure. The best way for youth to see through the artificialtiy and emptiness of our hedonistic culture is to experience the opposite through good family relationships."

God commands parents in Deuteronomy 6:6-9, to teach their children godliness form morning to night and at all times.

It is essential to take time with your child and discuss the issue of rock and roll. Show him the consequences. Explain the lifestyles of the rock stars. Point out the obituaries of the rock stars. The average age of their lifetime is in the mid-twenties. Scores have died through accidents related to alcohol drug overdose and suicide. You can read of over 100 obituaries telling of the death of rock stars in the book *Why Knock Rock.*

The weakening of parental authority confuses children. They need to know their limitations. This is how they derive their security. Dr. James Dobson in his book, "Dare to Discipline" page 56, says "There is security in defined limits. When the home atmosphere is as it should be, the child lives in utter safety. He never gets in trouble unless he deliberately asks for it, and as long as he stays within the limits, there is mirth and freedom and acceptance. If it means the absence of boundaries, or that each child sets it's own boundaries, then I'm unlaterably opposed to it."

Make sure your child understands you are condemning sexual perversion, not sex in its correct manner as ordained by God. Also explain you are not against wholesome fun but against hedonism. You must replace the vaccum once your child decides to give up rock music. Replace this gradually as you introduce him to contemporary Christian music. Visit churches that hold concerts of this nature. Parents, we must sacrifice and give much of our time to our children.

D. *The Challenge of the Cults*

BEYOND! The word has certain appeal. It makes one think of new horizons, new experiences! We are living in a time when many are attempting to move beyond God and His will for our lives. Here lies new danger.

The prevailing emotion of our civilization is not love or hate; it is boredom. People are demanding new fascinations to feed their ever-shortening spans of interest. The demand for new fascinations has led many beyond the faith once delivered to the saints to something newer and more exciting.

People envision God as living behind a stone wall — unreachable, untouchable. Actually God has invited us in to join His family, to be His children. There is nothing higher, greater or more magnificent than being a child of God. To try to move beyond this is dangerous. Once an individual moves beyond Christianity to the spirit realm, he leaves God and falls into a bottomless pit of heresy.

Cultists, humanists, and spiritists are all attempting to reach out beyond Christianity. In his book, *Know the Marks of the Cults*, David Breese observes:

Beyond rationality is insanity
Beyond medicine is poison
Beyond sex is perversion
Beyond fascination is addiction
Beyond love is lust
Beyond reality is fantasy
Beyond Christianity is death, hopelessness, darkness, heresy

What Is a Cult?

A cult is a religious perversion. It is a belief and practice in the world of religion which calls for devotion to a religious view or leader — usually a leader centered in false doctrine. A cult distorts the word of God by perverting the truth into a lie.

Cult leaders generally claim to have received a special revelation from God, possibly even continued revelations. This claim makes it difficult to discuss any part of the revealed word of God in reasonable terms.

Discussion with members of cults is extremely difficult because they are very well conditioned or brainwashed on how to relate to outsiders. The most bewildering thing about them is their claim to be freed from religious exploitation for they are carbon copies of their leader. The fact of the matter is that cultists have no freedom of speech. One either accepts what the leader says or is ostracized. Most cults are dogmatic and highly intolerant if their teachings are not accepted.

Why the Growth of Cults?

There are three primary reasons for the current surge of cults. The first is the fact that insecurity is one of life's major problems. Cult leaders know this and capitalize on it. When an insecure preson suddenly meets a group of people who seem happy, caring and loving, he or she naturally wants to be a part of it. Appearance does not matter, only feelings. This way of thinking can easily be explained because everything about today seems strange and different from any previous age. Man has lost his sense of security so he turns to myths. "For the time is coming when people will not endure sound teaching, but having itching ears they will accumulate for themselves teachers to suit their own likings, and will turn way from listening to the truth and wander into myths" (II Tim. 4:3,4).

The second reason is that this is a time of confusion. Values are questioned, traditional ideas are not acceptable but new ideas are unclear. This feeling is reflected in popular music. The lyrics of songs advocate free sex, devil worhsip, homosexuality, a please yourself attitude. Television programming is conditioning us to accept promiscuity as a way of life. The devil has convinced the world that if it feels good it must be right. Cults like Children of God advocate the latter philosophy.

The third reason for growth of cults is the need for human community. We all need to feel wanted, loved, useful. With our American emphasis on individual achievement we have lost a sense of community among people. As communities and schools become larger there is less and less communion between people. Independence, distrust, fences, isolation — it is a natural progression. Americans are becoming more and more isolated from one another and they long for that feeling of belonging to a caring community where wounds can be bandaged and happiness shared. This atmosphere provides a wonderful opportunity for the cultists.

The cults are bound together in a tight-knit community. One of their most marked features is the way members of the cults are deeply conscious of their community relationship. There is a deep sense of commitment coupled with an obvious caring for one another. I believe this is where the church has failed. The cults know this and have focused on it.

Understanding the Cults

It is important that we understand the mind of the cults. Usually a cult springs up around a powerful and overwhelming personality, for example, Mary Baker Eddy of Christian Science and C.T. Russell of the Jehovah Witnesses. Checking into the background of a cult leader usually provides helpful insights into the cult activities and beliefs. Joseph Smith had been a freemason and was removed from the Masonic Lodge. That fact helps to explain some of the Mormon ritualistic structure. Rev. Moon had a Christian background in the Presbyterian Church in Korea. He drifted from it into pentecostalism and then into anti-communist activities.

Cults usually center around the leader and often the cult dies when the leader dies. But what about those cults that live on? The reason they continue is because the writings of the deceased leader are accepted as gospel. The founder is then classified as messianic and is placed on a pedestal to the point of adoration and worship. Even though the writings and ideas of the founder of the cult contradict the word of God they are accepted. The Scriptures are then twisted and in some cases the Bible is relegated to a position below the writings of the founder. A classic example is the Book of Mormon. This is given precedence over the Word of God.

Cult organizations usually have a rigid set of teachings and lifestyles in which every member must abide. There is absolutely no room for freedom of thought of expression. Rigidity is necessary for the cult to exist. A cultist is dedicated to his belief and will absolutely refuse to have his teachings questioned.

Cult members will appeal to Christians on the authority of the Bible, usually their own translation. A poor student of God's word can easily become confused and uncertain. This opens the door for a foreign seed to be planted in the mind of the victim. The member of the cult who approaches you will not only bring mere words but a lifestyle that affirms the depth of his commitment.

The commitment of the Mormon young men to dedicate two years of their life evangelizing is an example of their dedication to their cause. These are requirements that are built in their lifestyle. When a cult member goes out into the streets to evangelize, he is proving his self worth. He is encouraged and praised by his peers for his effort.

What Can We Do?

(1) Christians today need to heed Peter's urgent call, "Always be prepared to make a defense to anyone who calls you to account to the hope that is in you. Yet do it with gentleness and reverence" (I Pet.

3:15). Cult leaders and followers alike know their message. We must know ours. Be committed.

(2) Remember that in an argument with a cultist, logic most likely will not prevail. These people usually believe their leader gets his information directly from God.

(3) Gather information about the cult. Know the leader's background and goals of the cults. Ask intelligent, specific questions.

(4) Approach the matter with prayer. Be patient. Leave the door open for a lost loved one to return. Be sure to let the individual know that even though you may not agree with what he is doing you still love him.

E. *The New Age Movement*

What the New Age Movement Is

In the past ten years the phenomenon known as the New Age Movement has shifted out of the counterculture born in the tumultuous sixties into the mainstream of society. Its effects are felt today in almost every aspect of life — medicine, politics, science, entertainment, psychology, and even religion. Although "New Age" is a term now commonly heard by the average person, there is still much uncertainty as to just what it means and what the New Age Movement is all about.

The New Age Movement is a vast network of like-minded worldwide organizations that aspire to, and may actually have the potential to achieve, the radical changing of western culture and mankind's understanding of his spirituality and his relationship to God. Its leaders invariably advocate Eastern philosophies and occultic practices. Its millions of sincere supporters have a common ecumenical basis — the belief in the oneness of all life and the divinity of man. They fervently believe that as each individual becomes aware of this unity of all things and the divinity within himself, an awakening of brotherhood and love such as never seen before will occur and an age of enlightenment, prosperity, and peace will dawn on the earth.

With this admirable goal in mind, followers earnestly work to win disciples, to disseminate their beliefs into the everyday life experiences of others — especially the young, and to bring about the changes in modern man's consciousness that they claim will herald the return of the True Messiah to earth. The "Messiah" they refer to is not Jesus Christ, nor any other external "god" descending to men, but rather it is the state of higher consciousness, or "Christ-consciousness," as it is called, available to every man which once collectively achieved will usher in the new Kingdom — that heaven on earth is made possible because spiritual men "will have developed god-like qualities and sufficient knowledge and wisdom to cooperate with God (the universal energy force) in materializing the Kingdom of God on earth" (John Randolph Price, *The Planetary Commission*).

What It Teaches

The New Age Movement draws from many sources — Eastern Mysticism, Occultism, the new self-actualizing psychologies, and the human potential movement. There is great diversity of beliefs and principles among New Agers as a result. However, certain foundational teachings run through all these different facets of the movement:

Monism (an element of Eastern religions)

This is the teaching that all that is, is one. Ultimately there is no difference between God and created things. Everything is part of one continuous reality that has no boundaries or divisions. Any perceived differences, such as good and evil, or separation of entities, are only apparent and not real. That very sense of separateness or difference is, in fact, a delusion to be overcome.

The Bible clearly refutes this in its presentation of God's creation as a diversity of objects, events, and persons. Creation is not a homogenous soup of undifferentiated unity but a complex plurality. God Himself is most definitely identified as a separate personality, an external Creator and Supreme Being.

Pantheism (another tenet of Eastern Mysticism)

This is the belief that all things — plant, animal, or inanimate — partake of one divine essence. All is one; all is god. Whatever is, is god and is therefore perfect. The idea of a personal God with a personality of His own is abandoned in favor of an impersonal energy force or consciousness. if all is one, then there is ultimately only one being — the One.

Again, the Bible affirms that all is not God. God the Creator stands undeniably and transcendentally distinct from His creation; Creation does not contain Him. The apostle Paul spoke very harshly against those who "exchanged the truth of God for a lie, and worshiped and served created things rather than the Creator" (Rom. 1:25).

Man Is God

This is one of the most seductive claims of the New Age. Man is depicted as evolving toward divinity through successive reincarnations which bring him ever closer to the conscious awareness that he is, in fact, the very god he seeks.

Listen to the words of Shirley MacLaine, perhaps the movement's most well-known and influential spokesperson: "You are everything. You are the universe. Man is the co-creator with god of the cosmos. You must never worship anyone or anything other than self. For you are god. To love self is to love god. The total understanding and realization of myself might require eons for me to accomplish, but when that awareness is achieved, I will be aligned completely with that unseen Divine Force we call god. For me to deny that Divine Force now, would be tantamount to denying that I exist. I know that I exist, therefore I AM. I know that the god-source exists, therefore, IT IS. Since I am a part of that force, then I AM THAT I AM."

This arrogant claim to a title used exclusively by the God of the Bible in reference to Himself, is obvious evidence of Satan's continued efforts to dethrone the Lord of Glory from the center of men's worship. He may be playing with new pawns (or New Age pawns) but his game is the same as of old.

The Need for Change of Consciousness

All is one; all is god; we are god. Then why don't we know ourselves as god? Our problem is ignorance. Western culture and Christianity have shaped our consciousness, moulding our experience and stifling our inherent psychic powers. We live under the everyday illusion of human limitations and finite abilities, looking outside ourselves to an exterior Creator-Being for strength and assistance. We need to be enlightened because we have forgotten our true identity.

The New Age Movement offers us relief from this metaphysical amnesia. Through techniques designed to alter ordinary consciousness, we can open the "doors of perception" so that we can see the true reality. There are many names for this transforming experience: cosmic consciousness, god-realization, self-realization, enlightenment, getting it, illumination, Nirvana, and "at-one-ment," to name a few. And it is a must that mankind as a whole undergo this process before the New Age can begin. As a popular New Age radio program "New Dimensions" states, "It is only through a change of consciousness that the world will be changed. This is our responsibility." (These people have a mission!)

The Bible also talks of a need of change in the consciousness of man. But it states the dilemma of humanity as not being the ignorance of our true divinity, but of the reality of our sin. The problem, not the answer, lies within ourselves. Jesus said that out of our hearts proceed all manner of evil (Mark 7:21-23), and He did not teach "at-one-ment" with God, but ATONEMENT through the sacrificial death of His only Son.

The Bible warns us about becoming involved in spiritual things (and that, in effect, is what consciousness raising is all about) apart from Christ (see Acts 19:13-16). The New Age's appeal to psychic powers is a terribly dangerous flirtation with spiritual matters specifically forbidden by God (Lev. 19:26,31; Deut. 18:10-12). And with good reason. Those who participate in these things leave themselves wide-open to the demonic forces of the spiritual realm and are easily caught under their influence. When large numbers of people are involved in this sort of thing, the potential for the dissemination of false doctrines is enormous, as spirits use these willing "transmitters" to teach and instruct mortal men spiritual matters. It is not difficult to see the groundwork for a great deception being laid here.

The Source of the Teachings

Shirley MacLaine, whose use of "trance channelers" is well-documented in her autobiographical works, is quick to point out that New Age teachings of cosmic "oneness" and man's divinity are appearing consistently, almost simultaneously, all over the world through channelers of different nationalities and languages. (Trance channelers are nothing more than spirit mediums whose practices of consulting with the dead and calling up the spirits are detestable to God and strictly forbidden by Him.) She claims that spirit guides speak through these human transmitters. They describe themselves as disembodied spirits existing on an "astral plane" as they await further incarnations. Their purpose in communicating with men is to assist them to higher levels of consciousness and to thus shorten their cycles of reincarnation.

Other prominent leaders of the New Age Movement also talk of their involvement with and personal instruction by spirit guides. Benjamin Creme, whose full-page newspaper ad in 1982 announcing the imminent arrival of the "Christ," brought the existence of the New Age Movement into the public eye, communicates regularly with this "Christ," a spirit guide who identifies himself as Lord Maitreya. (Maitreya in Sanskrit means "friend.") Alice Bailey, an influential New Age thinker who advocated global unity and a world religious system, accredited her teachings to the personal instruction of the spirit guide known as Djhwal Khal, the Tibetan. Other spirit personalities we hear about today are Ramtha, Seth, and Lazaris, and there are countless more. Again and again, the teachings of these "spirit guides" surface as the beliefs and doctrines of the New Age Movement.

As Christians we know the true identity of these so-called spiritual mentors. They are the very servants of Satan, the angels who fell in rebellion with him and who now are chained in darkness till the end times. They are demons posing as the dead or as souls waiting to be incarnated once again. They are participants in Satan's grand scheme for the final deception of the world.

Eastern mysticism, an ancient religion that has long been recognized as the very antithesis of Christianity, has also been drawn upon as a primary source of spiritual instruction for the New Age. Maharishi Mahesh Yogi, and his popular TM technique, is an obvious example of the new-found acceptance of Eastern religious principles in the West. He encourages followers to "be still and know that you are god," a deliberate distrotion of Scripture. Werner Erhard, founder of the EST training, was heavily influenced by Eastern Mysticism in the formation of his philosophies and claims that "you're a god in your universe." The then-President of Mormon Church, Brigham Young, claimed in 1873 that, "The devil told the truth (about godhood). I do not blame Mother Eve. I would not have had her miss eating the forbidden fruit for anything," meaning that the knowledge she thereby ingested is part of the whole, the ONE, that we must all come to know before we can recognize our own potential godhood. And now David Spangler, a leading figure in the New Age Movement today, picks up on the perverted teaching and even goes so far as to say, "When man entered upon the pathway to self, he entered into a great creative adventure . . . of learning the meaning of divinity by accepting to himself the responsibility of a microcosmic world unto whom he is god . . . then he can say, 'I have fully and absolutely accepted the responsibility of who and what I am.' The being that helps man to reach this point is Lucifer, the angel of man's evolution."

There Is Nothing New Under the Sun

How interesting that a belief system that proclaims itself as the herald of the "New Age" is buying the same old bill of goods first sold to Adam and Eve thousands of years ago in the garden. Satan still seeks to usurp the honor and worship due God alone as he did then, and he will draw as many souls as he can into doing the same.

One of the chief tactics he will use, and is using, in the "New Age" will be to challenge Jesus' teachings that He was THE CHRIST and is the only way to the Father. He will also try to raise questions concerning the early Church fathers and the Scriptures they selected (or failed to select) as they compiled what we know as the Bible today. This is a direct attack on Christianity itself and the authority of Scripture. (More about this in a later issue.)

Jesus said of the end time, "Watch out that no one deceives you; for many will come in my name claiming, 'I am the Christ,' and will deceive many" (Matt. 24:4,5). If the "New Age" turns out in fact to be the "end of the age," we need to be ready to "hold out the Word of Life" to rescue some of those "many." As Christians we need to know and to share the truths entrusted to us for this very purpose.

F. *The Reality of Satanism in America*

The frequency of problems that are arising due to young people's involvement with the occult is absolutely frightening, and not only is this coming to the attention of ministries such as ours, but also to police, parents, and clergy nationwide.

The evidence of a growing number of Satan worshipers in this country who are actively doing their master's dirty work is becoming undeniable. In the interest of civil rights, as the United States has become a nation of free-thinkers and liberal lifestyles, the groundwork has been firmly laid for Satanic influence to gain a foothold among our young people. Far from being a people who once stood for decency and orthodox Christianity as true religion, Americans now find it faddish to explore any and all so-called pathways to God, and in doing so have made acceptable practices and philosophies denounced as outright evil only a generation ago.

Consider the following items: The University of California at Berkeley offers a degree in sorcery. Witchcraft is taught in public schools all around the nation under such titles as "Literature of the Supernatural." The Satanic Bible outsells the Holy Bible two to one in most college towns, and a hundred to one in some places. There are an estimated one million self-proclaimed practicing witches in America, with heavy concentrations in New York and Southern California. Occult practitioners in New York City are demanding civil rights legislation that will protect witchcraft as a formal religion. The best-known Satanist in the country, Anton LaVey, who openly runs his Church of Satan in San Francisco, is frequently sought out by the entertainment industry as a technical advisor for music and films promulgating the occult. It has long been observed that much of today's music and film endorses the occult.

The stage has been amply set. Is it any wonder that we now face the phenomenon of young adults, teenagers, and even adolescents in growing numbers joining the ranks of those who commit unspeakable acts and actually serve the Devil? As fantastic or fanatical as this statement may seem to some, headlines occuring with increasing frequency in newspapers from all over the country bear witness that it is so.

The Daily News

Here is a sampling of crimes reported in newspapers that are the result of occultic activity. In the summer of 1985, Richard Ramirez (better known as the Night Stalker throughout the residential Southern California neighborhoods that he terrorized) ellegedly perpetrated fourteen murders. As he was sworn-in in a Los Angeles courtroom, his upraised palm displayed the five-pointed star in a circle positioned with two points up that symbolizes the Devil's horns. Horrible details concerning bizarre ritualistic multilations of his victim's bodies, as well as Satanic graffiti left on the walls at some of the crime scenes, added to the repugnance of his crimes. And most significantly, his description of how his reign of terror was an *acting out* of the lyrics of the Satanic rock band AC/DC reawakened echoes of another infamous Satan worshiper who had rained bloodshed and massacre on Southern California, Charles Manson.

Recently in Carl Junction, Missouri, three teenagers were charged with first degree murder in the death of a classmate beaten with baseball bats and dumped into a cistern. The three 17-year-olds told their attorneys that they thought they would somehow be rewarded by Satan. All three boys were deep into heavy metal music.

Scarcely a month later a fifteen-year-old girl from Vermont put a rifle to her head and killed herself. The lyrics to a heavy metal song were the last entry in her personal journal and a suicide note stated that she worshiped the Devil.

Shortly after this tragic incident, a 14-year-old boy from Newark, New Jersey, fatally stabbed his mother with a Boy Scout knife and then slit his own throat and wrists. His parochial school teachers had alerted his parents that he had been caught dabbling in Satanism. The boy had also told his friends of visions of Satan and was obsessed with Satanic literature and heavy metal music.

In Monroe, Michigan, the murder of a 17-year-old who was shot and killed on "Witches' Sabbath," a traditional day for human scrifice in Satanic circles, touched off the discovery of a devil worship cult among the *students at the local high school.*

One newspaper article, dated August, 1986, listed the following crimes:

In Maine, the jailed 18-year-old killer of a 12-year-old girl, left behind drawings that combined heavy metal music themes with Satanism. In Huntington Beach, California, thirty-three small animals kept in an elmentary schoolyard were slaughtered, a

198

crime that police say was apparently part of a Satanic ritual. In Contra Costa County, California, the battered body of a 17-year-old boy who had graduated from playing "Dungeons and Dragons" to being involved with a Satanic coven was found dead at the bottom of a cliff. He had told his father and others that he wanted to leave the group. Scores of reports link child molestations and disappearances to Satanic rituals featuring chalices of blood and participants either nude or wearing black hoods. Eight hundred crimes now under investigation by police nationwide are said to be linked somehow to Devil worship (The *Salisburg Post*, Aug. 22, 1986).

I believe that the number of these incidents is increasing, as the volume of consultations I am asked to give in this area indicates. The Chicago-based Cult Awareness Network reports that at least 10% of the 250 calls they receive each month are about teenagers involved in crime linked to Devil worship. The problem is becoming so serious that police authorities who once scoffed at the notion of an underground Satanic element operating in this country now conduct special seminars for other lawmen and psychologists to equip them to recognize and deal with this phenomenon. People who once feared to be called "witch-hunters" are now speaking out about what they know to be taking place in everyday suburban America. Denials of its existence ring hollow as the evidence mounts. Satanism is alive and well in the United States and *our children* are becoming its chief perpetrators *and* victims.

Why this "Fatal Attraction"?

The reasons for the current widespread occultic revival are many and complex. Some are sociological in nature, reflecting the spiritual state of the culture as a whole. Factors identified as contributing to this aspect of the issue are as follows:

The influence of Eastern religions which tend to mix any and all beliefs into one melting pot.

The prevailing attitude created by progress in psychic and para-psychological research holding that the occult is really a science.

The lack of governmental control over media, entertainment, and commercial products that espouse the occult.

The demise of traditional Christian theology and the watering down of Scriptural authority.

And perhaps most importantly, the *reality* of the occult, itself, coupled with the failure of people to discern the source of the supernatural forces they encounter.

As interesting as these factors are, to really understand the appeal of this evil we must see how individuals are drawn into its power.

The Young and the Restless

As with all preceding generations throughout history, this one has had to grapple with the rebelliousness of youth. Indeed, it is an essential part of the process of growing to adulthood. But in the modern world the pressures felt by our young people are far greater than ever before. They have grown up under the threat of world-annihilation. Mass media encourages sexual activity long before they are ready for it and morality has been dealt a heavy blow by the secular humanism they have been exposed to all their lives. Traditional religions have been altered, replaced, or abandoned altogether. The physical and emotional changes of puberty begin earlier, thanks to the high medical standards we have reached, but the message the adult world sends them is to hold back from finding a biological mate until "after college," a good ten years after their biological impulses begin. The structure and fabric of the family, as past generations have known it, has crumbled. Divorce, sexual disease, and homosexuality are rampant. Materialism reigns supreme and "the guy who dies with the most toys wins."

Our children are hurting and confused and angry; they are ripe for the picking and Satan is a skilled harvester. By offering earthly pleasures to divert the troubled minds of our youth, and mystical, supernatural powers and experiences to appease their soul-hunger, he draws them in like flies to the honey.

The Bait: Drugs, Sex, and Power

In his book, *The Satan Seller*, Mike Warnke, a former Satanist high priest, describes the usual route by which new candidates were led to inducement into Satanism. Almost invariably, the first lure was sex and plenty of it. Orgiastic parties, where Satan or the occult were never mentioned, were a common practice and the sex that was freely provided there became addictive; so, too, the drugs that were made available at these parties, seemingly for no cost. In reality, the cost turned out to be very high, for as a subject became more and more addicted to the gratification of these physical cravings, he was gradually led to understand that his service to the "Master" was required in order to keep his needs supplied.

Also, if a candidate seemed exceptionally promising, he could be enticed with the power of control over these commodities. This, of course, brought large amounts of money to the individual. A special select few, such as Warnke himself, were then invited to become involved at a much deeper level in which they actually learned Satanic rituals for casting spells and summoning demons. This ultimate power trip held Warnke in its grip for several years.

As he reached higher position within the coven and led his followers to increasingly more perverted rituals, including eating the flesh of severed fingers sacrificed to Satan by drug-frenzied cult members, Warnke began to have pangs of conscience (much to his own surprise) and fell from grace with the coven. When he decided to leave Satanism he was persecuted and threatened by the coven and it was only by turning to Christ that he was eventually delivered from their reach.

Warnke's experience is typical of those who try to disentangle themselves from Satan's clutches. However, he was more fortunate than most who try to escape. Those who do not know that they can run to Jesus Christ for forgiveness and for cover most often wind up dead at the hands of their former brothers. As always, Satan's path is one of hatred and violence and leads only to death. And *that* is what we must make our young people understand.

Parents! What to Look For

Because it is so difficult to be freed from the enticements and powers of Satanism, just as with cancer of the body, early detection can help to stop this malignancy of the spirit. The following are possible evidences that your child may be tampering with Satanism.

Although some children give no outward appearance that anything is wrong (as was the case for both the 15-year-old suicidal girl and the young boy who killed his mother as well as himself) certain music, books, personal writings, and paraphernalia warrant your attention and immediate discussion with your child.

Heavy Metal Music: Over and over again this music has been found to have influenced the minds of those who commit Satanistic crimes. Particular artists to watch for are KISS (Knights In Satan's Service), AC/DC, Ozzie Osborne, Black Sabbath, David Lee Roth, Alice Cooper, and Twisted Sister. There are countless more. A walk through your local record store and a look at some of the record jackets you'll find there should help you to identify others. There is even a category designated as "Satan Rock" in some of the more extensive stores.

Personal Effects: Jerwelry in the form of a goat's head, Satan is often depicted as a god with a man-like body but with the legs and head of a goat. Be particularly watchful for rings bearing the "symbol of the left hand," with its palm facing forward showing a pentagram and crescent in the center. This is a ring of initiation into a coven and is worn only to ceremonies and rituals. Sometimes amulets and zodiac signs are worn. More obvious tokens may be the number 666, a universally known symbol of Satan, or broken or inverted crosses, longtime favorites of Satan worshipers, symbolizing their hope that the power of the cross be broken. Also, pentagrams and black clothing should raise suspicion.

Occult Books: In particular the *Satanic Bible*, authored by Church of Satan founder Anton LeVay, Watch also for a "Book of Shadows," sometimes just a simple spiral notebook where kids record rituals, violent song lyrics, Satanic symbols, and suicide notes, all clues to the internal destruction taking place. Other books may cover such topics as the paranormal, the metaphysical, curses and spells, sexual deviations, and drugs. There is a wide range of topics included in the occult world.

Games: In particular, the Ouija Board and "Dungeons and Dragons." Also, anything that encourages fantasizing or roleplaying about magical or mystical powers.

Paraphernalia: Makeshift altars set up in bedrooms, candles, ritual knives, skulls and bones. Some rob graveyards to get what they need.

Drugs: The connection between Satanism and drugs cannot be over-stressed. Drugs are a primary tool of Satanic elements in performing rituals, in enticing new prospects, in controlling their followers, and in generating the inestimable cash flow that keeps the entire network afloat.

Personality Changes: Kids tend to be become more and more isolated and their grades drop drastically. They become argumentative and hostile to family and friends, and may even hang out with a new crowd. Some give themselves Satanic names.

Physical Signs: Marks of mutilation on body or arms. Satan demands blood sacrifices from his followers. Often this takes the form of animal sacrifices, but eventually disciples will offer their own blood. Nude women are used as the altars on which these sacrifices take place and they sometimes suffer injury as a result.

Teach Your Children Well

Parents, if you have a young person that you suspect is involved in the nightmare of Satanism, please share this article with him. Watch your local newspapers for stories that bring home the results of getting caught in this terrible web. Evidences of this sort abound all around us. The results of dabbling into the occult are always, ultimately death. Satanism bears the fruit of its master: lies, deceit, sexual promiscuity, unwanted pregnancies, abortion, drug addiction, alcoholism, sexual disease such as AIDS, fear, hate, violence, suicide, murder (and the really frightening thing about this is that it could be either done *to* you or *by* you or *both*), and most tragically, after all this earthly suffering — eternal spiritual death.

Paul's instruction to the Ephesians to understand the nature of the spiritual warfare being waged on this earthly plane for men's souls is vital, "For we wrestle not against flesh and blood, but against the rulers, against the authorities, against the powers of this dark world and against the spiritual forces of evil in the heavenly realms" (Eph. 6:12). We need to clearly understand the nature of our adversary, but we need also to understand the nature of our Advocate, Jesus Chirst, Our Risen Savior.

We must instruct our children that Jesus will always forgive and embrace even the most vile sinners. Nothing can separate us from His love if we truly seek His face. And it is His Holy Spirit that will comfort, strengthen, and deliver them back from the Evil One. And most importantly, we must pray for them. This is our greatest offensive weapon.

Satan is a formidable foe, indeed, when we believe his lies that say God will not have us. But as long as we remember the truth of God's promises to protect and defend us, to love and forgive us, and to eventually bring us to His side for eternity, we will have the strength to fend off Satan's fiery darts. This is the hope we hold out to our children and to all the world for "Greater is He that is in us than he who is in the world" (I John 4:4).

14

PUTTING ON THE WHOLE ARMOUR OF GOD

The Holy Spirit

In the book of Ephesians chapter 6:10-18 the Apostle Paul explains in a clear and concise manner who the enemy is. He then encourages us to put on the whole armour of God to resist the devil.

The person who helps us to accomplish this task is the Holy Spirit Himself. Jesus said, "But I tell you the truth, it is to your advantage that I go away; for if I do not go away, the Helper shall not come to you; but if I go, I will send Him to you" (John 16:7).

The Ministry of the Holy Spirit to the Believer

During my early years as a Christian, the Holy Spirit's place in my life was not explained to me. It seemed that the work of the Holy Spirit was always enshrouded in mystery. The Scripture gives some clear ideas of the work of the Spirit. It is the intention of this final section to draw attention to them.

The Spirit Dwells within the Believer

On the day of Pentecost, the crowd cried out, "Brethren, what shall we do?" Peter replied, "Repent, and let each of you be baptized in the name of Jesus Christ for the forgiveness of your sins; and you shall receive the gift of the Holy Spirit" (Acts 2:38). The gift wasn't from the Holy Spirit; the Holy Spirit was the gift. When the twelve apostles were arrested in Jerusalem and put on trial before the Sanhedrin, Peter replied with great courage, "We must obey God rather than men. The God of our fathers raised up Jesus whom you had put to death by hanging Him on a cross. He is the one whom God exalted to His right hand as a Prince and Saviour, to grant repentance to Israel, and forgiveness of sins. And we are witnesses of these things, and so is the Holy Spirit, whom God has given to those who obey Him" (Acts 5:29-32). Here Peter said that the Holy Spirit is given to those who obey. In I Corinthians 6:19, Paul wrote, "You are not in the flesh but in the Spirit, if indeed the Spirit of God dwells in you."

In Romans 8:11, Paul said, "If the Spirit of Him who raised Jesus from the dead *dwells in you*, He who raised Christ Jesus from the dead wil also give life to your mortal bodies through His Spirit who dwells in you."

What Does the Holy Spirit Do?

It is often said, "I have heard all of my life that the Holy Spirit dwells within us. However, what does He do? How does He work?" These are fair questions. The Bible provides the answers.

The Holy Spirit Is a Source of Spiritual Life

Jesus Christ said that "He who believes in me, as the Scripture said, 'From his innermost being shall flow rivers of living water.' But He spoke of the Spirit, whom those who believed in Him were to receive" (John 7:38,39). Here we see that the Holy Spirit is a source of spiritual life.

The Holy Spirit Brings about Conviction of Sin

The Holy Spirit brings about conviction of sin (John 16:8). There were many times as I was driving my cab in London when I would be convicted of a sin I had committed the night before. I would tell God I was sorry and ask Him to forgive me. Very often I would go to a church, get down on my knees and tell God how sorry I was. Then I would make up my mind that I was going to be a good person. As I got back into my taxi I would say, "God, I am going to behave myself." My repentance didn't last long, though. Five or ten minutes later as I was driving along, I would see someone and thoughts would come into my mind. Before I realized it I was sinning in my thoughts. There are some questions we must ask ourselves: (1) Why was I convicted in the first place? (2) How was I convicted? (3) Why couldn't I do right?

(1) Our faith does not come by feeling, it comes by hearing. I was convicted by the Word of God. As a little Jewish boy I had learned the ten commandments. I knew I was breaking some of those commandments. I knew what God expected of me and I knew I was not living up to it.

(2) The Spirit was convicting me through the Word. Even though I was not Christian and did not know what God expected under the new covenant, I did know the law and I knew I was breaking it.

(3) My breaking of the law continued because I did not have the person of the Holy Spirit dwelling in my life. It was my flesh versus Satan and I was lost. It wasn't until I became a Christian and had the Holy Spirit dwelling in me that I could win. "Greater is He who is in you (the person of the Holy Spirit) than he (Satan) that is in the world" (I John 4:4).

The Holy Spirit Provides Strength to Meet Temptation

Now what good would it be if a man should gain the forgivenenss of sins and then fall back and become enslaved in sin again? This is why God has arranged us help through the person of the Holy Spirit. In Ephesians 3:16, Paul says that it is possible for us to be strengthened with might through His Spirit in the inner man. The indwelling Spirit strengthens us and helps us to overcome temptation and sin. We need help in our struggles with Satan. We cannot do it on our own. In Romans 7, Paul describes his struggle against Satan. He mentions the personal pronoun, "I" thirty-two times. He did everything possible to overcome sin, and yet he failed. he cried out in desperation, "Wretched man that I am! Who will set me free from the body of this death?'' Romans 8 shows the answer to his problem. It is no longer Paul versus the flesh; it is the Spirit versus the flesh. That is why Paul says, "There is therefore now no condemnation to those who are in Christ Jesus" (Rom. 8:1). Why? "We walk not after the flesh but after the Spirit." The Holy Spirit works within us more than we think. Many times Scriptures flash through our minds reminding us of the dangers and the consequences of sin, and showing us the possibilities of escape (I Cor. 10:13). The Spirit, occupies our minds with thoughts that are true, honorable, pure, lovely, and of good report (Phil. 4:8).

I remember one occasion when Satan was tempting me. I was driving in my car and a particular sin came before me. Satan seemed to be saying, "This is not really a sin, and you are strong." It was beginning to bother me. After all, I knew sin could be a pleasure but the wages of sin is death. Thoughts flashed through my mind as though Satan was talking to me, saying, "Even if you do sin you can turn to I John 1:9 and confess your sins and he will forgive you." At the same time it seemd there was someone else there who was saying, "Yes, but Hebrews 10:26 says that if you continue to willfully sin there is no more sacrifice for you." It was a strange feeling I had as I drove along. It seemed there were three personalities, Satan on the one side, the Holy Spirit on the other and my mind the battle ground. As all these thoughts were passing through my mind, a strange thing happened. I believe the providence of God manifested itself here. The car radio was on, and as the music finished a minister began speaking. He said, "I want to leave you with a thought for the day. If you want to avoid the fruits of sin, stay out of the orchard." I thought, "Praise the Lord," pressed my foot down on the accelerator, and went straight out of the orchard.

The apostle Paul tells us in Ephesians 6:12, "For our struggle is not against the flesh and blood, but against the rulers, against the powers, against the world forces of this darkness, against the Spiritual forces of wickedness in the heavenly places." Our mind is the battleground, but we are the ones who make the decision. We have control. Many of us get trapped in sin because we resist the Spirit, by wanting our own desires (Acts 7:51).

Romans 8:13 says, "If you are living according to the flesh, you must die, but if by the Spirit you are putting to death the deeds of the body, you will live." God has offered us the Holy Spirit as a continuous scource of spiritual strength in order that we might live a life that is honorable to Him.

The Holy Spirit Helps Us Pray   Our prayers are often selfish. God said He would provide all needs but not all our wants. The Holy Spirit knows what is best for us and can make our prayers acceptable to God (Rom. 8:26,27).

There are times we have been under emotional stress and are so burdened down we don't know how to pray. When we feel so inadequate the Spirit takes our prayers before God and petitions for us in such a way that our prayers become a might force.

The Holy Spirit Guarantees Eternal Life

The Holy Spirit is given to us as a pledge of eternal life. "For we know that if the earthly tent which is our house is torn down, we have a building from God, a house not made with hands, eternal in the heavens. . . . He who has prepared us for this very purpose is God who gave to us the Spirit as a pledge" (II Cor. 5:1,5). Paul says we are sealed with the promise of the Holy Spirit (Eph. 1:13-14). The Holy Spirit has given us this pledge and when we leave this earth He will deliver the full inheritance.

Our Lord told us He would not leave us as orphans. He sent us the person of the Holy Spirit. He is our comforter, our protector. Satan said it well, (not that he wanted it to be so) in his discussion with God about Job, Satan said, "Hast not thou made an hedge about him, and about his house, and about all that he hath on every side? thou has blessed the work of his hands, and his substance is increased in the land" (Job 1:10).

God has put a hedge around the Christians and we must never forget that "Greater is He that is in you than he that is in this world" (I John 4:4). Amen.

SCRIPTURES RELATING TO THE OCCULT

Astrology
Isaiah 47:13
Daniel 1:20; 2:2, 10, 27; 4:7; 5:7, 11, 15
Deuteronomy 4:19; 17:3
II Kings 17:16; 21:3, 5
Jeremiah 8:2; 19:13
Zephaniah 1:5
Acts 7:42, 43
II Chronicles 33:3, 5

Drugs or Pharmakeia
Revelation 21:8; 22:15

Familiar Spirits or Mediums
Leviticus 19:31; 20:6; 20:27
Deuteronomy 18:11
I Samuel 28:3, 7, 8, 9
II Kings 21:6; 23:24
I Chronicles 10:13
II Chronicles 33:6
Isaiah 8:19; 19:3; 29:4

False Prophets and Signs and Wonders
Matthew 12:39; 24:24
II Thessalonians 2:9-11
Revelation 13:13; 16:14

Divination
Numbers 22:7; 23:23
Deuteronomy 18:10
II Kings 17:17
Jeremiah 14:14; 29:8
Ezekiel 12:24; 13:6, 7; 21:22, 23
Acts 16:16

Witchcraft
I Samuel 15:23
II Chronicles 33:6
Galatians 5:20
II Kings 9:22
Micah 5:12
Nahum 3:4

Wizards
Leviticus 19:31; 20:6, 27
Deuteronomy 18:11

Witches
Exodus 22:18
Deuteronomy 18:10

Sorcery
Exodus 7:11
Isaiah 47:9, 12; 57:3
Daniel 2:2
Acts 8:9, 11
Revelation 9:21; 18:23

Soothsayer
Isaiah 2:6
Daniel 2:27; 4:7; 5:7, 11
Micah 5:12
Acts 16:16

Demons
Matthew 4:1, 5, 8, 11, 24; 8:31; 9:33; 12:22; 13:39; 15:22; 17:18; 25:41
Mark 5:12, 15, 16, 18; 7:29, 30; 16:17
Luke 4:2, 3, 5, 6, 13, 33, 35; 7:33; 8:12, 29, 36; 9:42; 11:14
John 6:70; 7:20; 8:44, 48, 49, 52; 10:20, 21; 13:2
Acts 10:38; 13:10
I Corinthians 10:20
Ephesians 4:27; 6:11
I Timothy 3:6, 7; 4:1
II Timothy 2:26
Hebrews 2:14
James 3:15; 4:7
I Peter 5:8
I John 3:8, 10
Jude 9
Revelation 2:10; 12:9, 12; 20:2, 10

For Further Information Write:
Exposing Satan's Power Ministries
P.O. Box 11029
St. Petersburg, Florida 33733